Reunited Hearts

Riya Gora

HAWK PRESS

Published by

Hawk Press
4836/24, Ansari Road, Daryaganj
New Delhi – 110 002
Phones : 9643330713, +91-11-23278618, +91-11-35676207
E-mail : thehawkpress@gmail.com
www.thehawkpress.com

Contents

"Even when nothing feels right, be patient — trust the timing and believe that something good is on its way."

PROLOGUE

During the bright days of their youth, the campus of St. Martin's College was like a kingdom for Eeshan, Aashi, Rohan, and Myra—four close friends who faced the challenges of growing up together. Their days were full of laughter, late-night study sessions, and dreams about the future. They were inseparable, each friend bringing something special to the group, making their bond strong and unique.

Eeshan was the dreamer, always lost in thoughts about a future full of endless possibilities. Aashi, with her contagious laughter and strong optimism, was the one who kept the group together. Rohan was passionate and sometimes acted without thinking, which led to disagreements with Eeshan, but their friendship remained strong. Myra, the quiet and thoughtful one, added calmness and a sense of reflection to their group.

However, as graduation approached, the pressures of adulthood started to strain their close-knit group. Small misunderstandings turned into bigger conflicts. Hurtful words were spoken in anger, leaving deep scars. One night, a serious argument broke their bond, and they drifted apart. The promise of their friendship faded into silence, and the once inseparable group disbanded.

Three years went by, with each friend following their own path. Eeshan threw himself into his career, chasing the dreams he once shared with his friends, but he always felt like something was missing. Aashi still smiled, but her eyes no longer sparkled the same way, as her heart carried the weight of regret. Rohan's fiery spirit led him on a rough journey, and he often found himself thinking about the friendships he had lost. Myra, with her quiet strength, built a life of her own, but she never forgot the friends who had once meant the world to her.

Life, with its unpredictable twists, decided their story wasn't over yet. By chance, they all returned to the city that had once been their playground. They crossed paths again, but this time they were no longer carefree college students. They were adults, carrying the memories and emotions of their shared past. When they met again, old feelings resurfaced—love, anger, regret, and a longing for the days they had left behind.

As they faced their past, the wounds that had never fully healed reopened. They wondered if they could forgive each other and rebuild the bridges they had burned. Could they handle the complexities of their relationships now that they had all changed so much? The city, now filled with memories of the past and the possibility of new beginnings, held the answers they were looking for.

As they spent time together again, they realized that the lines between friendship and love were not as clear as they once thought. They had to figure out what they truly meant to each other now. There was confusion and emotional turmoil, but one thing became clear: *some bonds, no matter how strained, are meant to last.*

Through these experiences, they learned that true friendship can survive even the toughest challenges. Though they had been apart for years, their bond was strong enough to bring them back together, showing that some connections are simply unbreakable.

1

THE REUNION

The college had announced a reunion, the same place where countless events and memories were made: the grand auditorium. It was decorated with twinkling lights and a big stage, a setting perfect for rekindling old friendships and reliving fond memories. Nervousness hung in the air as everyone anticipated meeting again after three long years. It was a mix of emotions—excitement, anxiety, and a whirlwind of thoughts. Little did they know how their lives were about to change.

The big, decorated gate of the auditorium remained empty until Eeshan stepped through. Tall, with striking brown eyes, he wore a perfect black suit, embodying the image of a true gentleman. He had grown into a successful man, now the proud owner of a renowned resort. His confident demeanor belied the nervousness in his eyes, which were searching the crowd, looking for someone. His heart raced as he scanned the room, until she walked in.

Aashi

Aashi entered, wearing a stunning lavender dress with a slit and high, shimmery heels. Her golden brown eyes and radiant smile made her look as youthful as she did in college, if not younger. Now a successful fashion designer, her elegance and poise were unmistakable. Yet, beneath her big smile, a hint of anxiety lingered. Her heart pounded as she spotted Eeshan and began to walk towards him, her mind flooded with memories of the past three years. Just as she was about to greet him, she collided with a waiter and slipped.

In a perfect Bollywood moment, Aashi was about to fall when a strong hand caught her. Her eyes were closed, bracing for the fall, but when she opened them, she was stunned to see Rohan. His bold eyes and confident demeanor were just as she remembered, but there was a newfound calmness about him. Now a successful engineer with a prominent IT company in Gurgaon, Rohan seemed different yet familiar.

For a moment, Aashi and Rohan were frozen in time until Eeshan tapped Rohan's shoulder, breaking the spell. Nervousness hung in the air as the three friends stood together, a mix of emotions swirling around them. These were the friends who had shared endless laughter and secrets, yet now they sensed a palpable tension. Despite this, they managed to exchange awkward hellos, trying to bridge the gap that had formed over the years.

Eeshan, Aashi, and Rohan had arrived, but there was one person missing: Myra. Would she come? Could they all sort things out? What had really happened three years ago? The questions lingered in the air, as the night of the reunion began to unfold.

2

MEMORIES REKINDLED

The auditorium buzzed with the excitement and nervousness of reunions as old friends caught up, sharing stories of where life had taken them. Eeshan, Aashi, and Rohan stood together, their initial awkwardness giving way to tentative smiles and polite conversation. Yet, each felt the weight of unresolved issues and the absence of Myra, their missing friend. Eeshan couldn't shake the feeling of nostalgia mixed with regret. As he glanced around, memories of their college days flooded back. He remembered the nights spent planning their futures, convinced their bond was unbreakable.

Flashback

Three years ago, on a similarly decorated stage, they had celebrated their graduation. The future seemed bright, and their friendship felt like it would last forever. But that night, a heated argument erupted, words were exchanged that couldn't be taken back, and their once-solid bond shattered .

Aashi recalled a night when they stayed up late, talking about their dreams. She shared her vision of becoming a fashion designer, and her friends encouraged her every step of the way.

Now, she wondered if they could ever regain that closeness.

Rohan felt a mixture of relief and unease. Saving Aashi from falling had felt instinctive, bringing back memories of his role as the group's protector. He had always defended his friends, but that night three years ago, he felt the most betrayed. The argument started over something trivial but escalated quickly, with Rohan storming out. Could they really move past it?

As they stood reminiscing, the door to the auditorium opened again. Myra walked in, her eyes scanning the room nervously. She looked absolutely changed, her personality - she looked more confident and beautiful . As she approached, the air grew thick with anticipation.

"Hey, everyone," Myra said softly, her voice a blend of warmth and uncertainty.

The group fell silent, each grappling with their emotions. Myra had always been the peacekeeper. Seeing her again brought a mix of hope and fear—hope that they could mend their friendships, and fear that too much damage had been done.

They began to talk, their conversation starting tentatively but soon easing into the familiar rhythm of their old friendship. Laughter and updates flowed, but underlying questions remained: Could they trust each other again? Were the wounds too deep to heal?

Suddenly, a familiar song played: *"Tu Hai To I Will Be Alright."* It was their go-to song. For a moment, they were lost in bittersweet nostalgia.

"Remember when we used to sing this at every party?" Aashi said, her voice tinged with both joy and sadness.

Rohan nodded. "Yeah, those were some good times."

Myra spoke up. "We've all changed. Maybe we should really talk, understand what happened, and see if we can move forward."

Her suggestion hung in the air. They knew this conversation was long overdue.

"Let's step outside," Eeshan suggested. "We need to talk without distractions."

They agreed and made their way outside, the cool night air heavy with the weight of the past. Under the stars, they prepared to confront their history, hoping to find a way forward.

3

CONFRONTING THE PAST

The night air was cool and crisp as Eeshan, Aashi, Rohan, and Myra stood in a quiet corner of the campus, away from the bustling reunion. The stars above seemed to bear silent witness to the tension that hung between them.

Eeshan was the first to speak, his voice low but steady. "We need to talk about what happened three years ago. I've carried the weight of that night for too long."

Rohan crossed his arms, his expression guarded. "So have I. But it's not just about what happened that night. It's about everything that led up to it."

Aashi nodded, her eyes filled with a mix of determination and apprehension. "We all made mistakes. But we need to understand each other's perspectives if we want to move forward."

Myra, always the mediator, took a deep breath. "Let's start from the beginning. What really happened between you two?"

Eeshan glanced at Rohan before turning to Aashi, taking a deep breath. "I need to come clean. I had feelings for you, Aashi. Seeing you spend so much time with Rohan made me jealous. I thought you two were... together. I let my emotions get the best of me, and I lashed out."

Aashi's eyes widened in surprise. She burst into tears. "Eeshan, I had no idea. I never meant to make you feel that way. Rohan and I were just working on that project."

Rohan's expression softened, though his frustration was still evident. "Why didn't you say anything, Eeshan? We were supposed to be honest with each other. I knew you liked her. Why would I see her that way? I treated her like my younger sister and maybe your would-be girlfriend," he added to lighten the atmosphere.

Everyone giggled except Aashi, who confronted Rohan. "You knew and still didn't tell me, Ro? Why?"

"I thought I would break the surprise of Eeshan proposing to you at the farewell. I didn't want to ruin it," explained Rohan.

Eeshan sighed, rubbing the back of his neck. "I was scared. Scared of ruining our friendship if I admitted how I felt. But then I saw you two together all the time, and I couldn't control my jealousy. I'm sorry for how I acted."

Rohan nodded slowly. "I understand. But it wasn't just about jealousy, was it? We were all under a lot of pressure, and I felt like you didn't trust me."

Aashi looked between her two friends, her voice earnest. "I'm sorry too. I should have noticed how you were feeling, Eeshan. I never meant to hurt either of you."

Myra stepped closer. "We all need to take responsibility for our actions. But what's important now is that we're here, willing to talk and understand each other."

Rohan took a deep breath. "I think we can move past this, but it will take time. We need to rebuild the trust that was broken."

Eeshan nodded. "Agreed. I'm willing to put in the effort if you all are."

Aashi smiled, though tears glistened in her eyes. "I want to fix this. We were always stronger together."

Myra placed a hand on Eeshan's shoulder. "We've all grown. We've learned from our mistakes. And now, we have a chance to start fresh."

"Let's make a pact," Myra suggested, her voice firm yet gentle. "To always be honest with each other from now on. No more secrets, no more misunderstandings."

Eeshan, Aashi, and Rohan nodded in agreement.

As they stood there, united once more, they felt the first steps toward healing. The journey ahead was uncertain, but they were ready to face it—together.

Friendship is not about whom you have known the longest, but about who came and never left your side.

Just as they were about to head back, Myra's phone buzzed with a message. She glanced at the screen and froze. "Guys, you won't believe who just texted me."

Eeshan, Aashi, and Rohan exchanged curious glances, their minds racing with possibilities.

"What is it, Myra?" Eeshan asked.

She looked up, her eyes wide with a mix of shock and excitement. "It's from someone we never expected to hear from again."

The mystery of the message hung in the air, leaving them all on edge. Who had reached out after all these years? And what could it mean for their newly mended friendship?

4

THE HAUNTING MESSAGE

The night after the reunion, the group decided to meet at a café near the campus. The atmosphere was a mix of nostalgia and tension as they awaited the arrival of the person behind the mysterious message. Each of them grappled with their own thoughts and questions, the unresolved past weighing heavily on their minds.

As they walked back from the reunion, Myra's phone buzzed again. She glanced down, eyebrows furrowing. "Guys, I just got another message. It's from Raj, my ex," said Myra as tears rolled down her face.

Rohan clenched his fists. "That scumbag? He's back?"

"Raj?" Eeshan asked. "What does he want?"

"Yes," Myra nodded, her voice shaky. "He wants to meet tonight at the old café near campus. But..."

Aashi noticed the fear in Myra's eyes. "What is it, Myra? What's wrong?"

Myra took a deep breath. "He's threatening me with false

pictures he made using AI. He's looking for revenge. I'm scared. You remember the day you beat him up badly for bullying me? Then he left the college. I thought I was safe, but now he's back again. I don't know what to do," cried Myra.

Eeshan placed a reassuring hand on her shoulder. "You're not alone, Myra. We'll face this together."

Later that evening, they gathered at the café, its warm, familiar ambiance a stark contrast to the anxiety they felt waiting for Raj. He arrived, wearing a smug smile, his eyes glinting with malice. "Hello, Myra. Long time no see."

Rohan stood up, his eyes blazing with anger. "What do you want, Raj?"

Raj smirked. "I just wanted to see my old friends. And remind Myra of our unfinished business."

Aashi glared at him. "You have no business here, Raj. Leave her alone."

Raj's smile widened as he pulled out his phone. "Oh, I think I do. See these? AI is a wonderful tool, isn't it? Imagine what these pictures could do to Myra's reputation."

Myra trembled, her friends surrounding her protectively. "What do you want?" she asked, her voice barely above a whisper.

Raj leaned in, his tone menacing. "I want Myra to suffer. I want her to know that she can never escape me."

Eeshan stepped forward. "We won't let you hurt her, Raj. Leave now, or we'll call the police."

Raj laughed. "Oh, I'm not scared of the police. But fine, I'll leave. For now. But remember, Myra, I'll always be watching."

As Raj walked away, the group sat back down. Myra was shaking, her fear evident.

Aashi turned to Myra, her voice filled with resolve. "We need to figure out how to stop him. We can't let him keep threatening you."

Rohan added, "And we'll stay with you, Myra. He won't get to you as long as we're here."

Myra wiped her tears, a small spark of hope in her eyes. "Thank you, guys. I don't know what I'd do without you."

As they devised a plan to protect Myra and gather evidence against Raj, they realized that their bond was stronger than ever. Together, they could face anything—even the ghosts of their pasts.

As they stood to leave, Myra's phone buzzed again. She hesitated before looking at it, her eyes widening in shock. "Guys, you need to see this."

Eeshan, Aashi, and Rohan crowded around her, their faces turning pale as they read the message. It wasn't just a threat—it was a countdown.

"Time's ticking, Myra. Make your choice. Tick-tock."

$$5$$

GAME OVER

The weight of Raj's haunting message hung heavily over the group as they gathered in Eeshan's apartment that night. The countdown had started, and the ticking clock added urgency to their discussions. They knew they had to act quickly and decisively to protect Myra and put an end to Raj's threats once and for all.

"We need to gather as much evidence as we can against him and go to the police. But first, we need to understand his game," said Eeshan.

Sitting on the sofa, biting her nails in stress, Aashi stood up. "Rohan, you're an engineer. Try to hack something, bro."

Rohan, ever the tech-savvy one, pulled out his laptop. "I can start by looking into the AI-generated images he's using. Maybe we can trace them back to their source."

Myra sat quietly, trying to steady her nerves. "I'm scared, but I know I can't face this alone. Thank you all for standing by me."

Eeshan placed a comforting hand on her shoulder. "We're in

this together, Myra. We always have been, and we always will be."

Everyone nodded in agreement. Rohan worked tirelessly on his laptop to rescue Myra from this scare.

As dawn approached, Rohan leaned back in his chair, a triumphant look on his face. "I've found something. Raj has been using specific software to create those images. If we can prove he's behind it, we can take this to the police."

Aashi's eyes lit up. "That's great news! What's our next step?"

Rohan pointed to the screen. "We need to get a hold of Raj's devices. If we can find this software on his computer or phone, it'll be undeniable proof."

Later that day, Raj sent another message to Myra, taunting her and demanding she meet him alone. This time, the group decided to confront him directly.

They arrived at the designated meeting spot—a park on the outskirts of town. Myra's hands trembled as she clutched her phone, but she stood tall, having her friends by her side.

Raj appeared, smirking. "I see you brought your little gang. How touching."

Myra stepped forward confidently. "It's over, Raj. We have evidence against you. Your game is over."

Rohan stepped in, holding up his phone. "We've traced the AI software you used. It's only a matter of time before the police trace it back to you."

Raj's smirk widened, showing no signs of fear. "You really think you can outsmart me? This is just the beginning. You have no idea what I'm capable of."

Aashi's determination didn't waver. "We're not backing down.

Stop this now, or we'll go to the police with everything we have."

Raj confidently said , "Do what you must. But remember, I always have the upper hand. I'm always watching."

As Raj walked away, his threat lingered in the air, leaving the group with a chilling sense of dread. They had taken the first step, but it was clear their fight was far from over.

The friends stood united, their resolve unshaken, ready to face whatever came next. The battle had only just begun, and they knew they needed to be prepared for anything.

6

READY TO FIGHT

The news that Raj wasn't acting alone made their situation urgent. "We need to find out who else is with him," Eeshan said firmly, breaking the silence. There was an uneasy tension in the air.

Rohan nodded seriously, typing quickly on his laptop. "Raj acts too confident to be acting alone. Someone else is pulling the strings."

Myra, looking scared but determined, said, "We have to stop this. It can't continue like this. It's not just about me anymore; it's about all of us. We need to stop them."

Aashi squeezed Myra's arm. "We're together in this, Myra. We'll find a way to end it. You are not alone." Rohan focused harder as he searched Raj's digital history . "I'm going to track every connection, every message. We need to find out who's behind all of this."

Eeshan called his tech contacts urgently, hoping for any clue about Raj's network. Finally, they got a lead.

"Raj's been talking to someone regularly. Maybe that's who's behind everything," Eeshan suggested, determined. "But how do we find this mystery person?"

Aashi had an idea. "My dad's friend, Inspector Varun, could help. But I'm worried about involving my parents..." Myra interrupted firmly, "No, we can't risk our families. It's too dangerous."

Eeshan thought for a moment. "What if we tell Inspector Varun part of the story and ask for his help quietly? He might understand and keep it confidential."

Myra tried to object, but Rohan put a finger on her lips softly, glanced at her, and said, "Shhh, trust me. We can do this. I assure you nothing will happen."

He focused back on his search and responded, "That's a smart move. It'll keep us safe and get us the help we need."

They turned to Myra, waiting for her decision to proceed with their risky plan.

"Okay," Myra finally agreed, her voice steady. "Let's do it. But we need to be careful every step of the way."

The next day, Aashi met with Inspector Varun, explaining their situation carefully and asking for his help discreetly. Inspector Varun listened seriously, his expression growing more serious with every detail about Raj's threats.

"This is serious," Inspector Varun said, looking at each of them. "I understand your concerns about your families. I'll handle this quietly."

Rohan leaned forward, urgent. "We need to find out who Raj's contact is. Any help you can give us will be important."

Inspector Varun nodded thoughtfully. "I'll start by looking into Raj's recent activities and contacts. If there's a pattern, we might find out who's working with him."

They discussed risks and strategies, planning how to gather evidence without attracting attention.

Back at Eeshan's place, they reviewed what they knew and planned their next move. Each clue pointed to a bigger scheme, bringing them closer to finding who was really behind Raj's actions.

As they talked about their next steps, Myra got a chilling message on her phone — a reminder that he was still watching.

The message was simple but threatening: "You're getting closer, but so am I."

Tension filled the room as they realized the danger was growing. Aashi glanced at Myra. "Are you okay? This must be so overwhelming for you."

Myra nodded, her voice trembling slightly. "It is. But knowing I have all of you with me gives me strength."

Rohan tapped away on his laptop, frustration evident in his furrowed brow. "We need more than strength. We need a breakthrough." Eeshan paced the room, his mind racing. "Varun mentioned he'd start with tracing Raj's recent activities. That could lead us to his accomplice."

Aashi checked her phone nervously. "I hope Varun finds something soon. Every moment we delay, Raj could be plotting his next move." Just then, a call interrupted their conversation. Aashi answered hesitantly, recognizing Varun's number. After a brief exchange, she hung up with a mix of relief and apprehension.

"He found something," Aashi announced, her voice tinged with urgency. "Raj has been communicating with a known cybercriminal, someone with ties to organized crime." Myra's heart sank, the weight of the revelation hitting her hard. "So, it's not just Raj. There's a whole network behind him and he was just faking the everything for money , i can't believe i trusted him ..how can i be so dumb "

Rohan closed his laptop with a determined thud. "We need to act fast. If we can get concrete evidence linking Raj to this cybercriminal, we can bring them both down." Eeshan nodded in agreement. "Varun said he'll gather more intel on the cybercriminal's whereabouts. Meanwhile, we need to prepare ourselves."

After some hours

As they strategized, their minds racing with the gravity of their mission. Finally, as dusk settled over the city, Aashi's phone buzzed again—a text from Varun. "He's tracked down the cybercriminal's location," Aashi read aloud, her voice quivering with anticipation. "He's willing to meet us tomorrow at a secure location."

Myra took a deep breath, her resolve hardening. "Tomorrow, we end this." "Will it finally end tomorrow?" Aashi wondered aloud, her voice filled with hope and apprehension.

Everyone stood in silence, each lost in their own thoughts about what the next day would bring. "I think you should try to get some rest," Rohan suggested gently. "You'll need all your strength tomorrow."

"I can't rest in this situation," Myra admitted, her voice tinged with weariness. "I was finally moving on in life, finally smiling again, and now he's back to ruin everything. Why does he keep coming back? Why is this happening to me?" Tears welled up in her eyes.

Rohan rushed to his room and returned with a guitar, playing a soothing melody that calmed Myra. He then hugged her, reassuring her of his presence and support. Aashi and Eeshan joined in the hug, their solidarity unspoken yet deeply felt.

"I promise you, Myra," Rohan said softly, "tomorrow, this will end. No more looking back." Myra managed a small smile, her gratitude evident in her eyes.

The next day

They all woke up with tension evident in their expressions. Today, they had to put an end to all of this and free Myra from this terror.

They all got ready to meet Inspector Varun for planning further action. He arrived at the location and said, "I have done a thorough check on the cybercriminal records and we have found out who it could be. His name is Ronnie and he has a history of cybercrimes. It won't be easy, but we can bring him down together."

He explained the plan to the group. "We will track his last location and reach there to gather evidence linking to him, but we need to be very cautious as it can be dangerous. We will spread out in pairs and stay in touch through calls."

It was time. The group, accompanied by Inspector Varun, went to the last seen location of Ronnie, an abandoned warehouse. They were scared but confident, knowing they had to end it today.

7

THE FINAL STAND

As they approached the warehouse, Varun signaled for silence. "We need to be very careful," he whispered. "Follow my lead."

Inside the warehouse, they found evidence of a large-scale operation—computers, files, and traces of cyber activity. It was clear that Ronnie was planning something big.

Suddenly, a noise echoed through the warehouse. They turned to see a figure emerging from the shadows—it was Ronnie, and three of his gang members.

"Well, well, look who decided to drop by," Ronnie sneered, his eyes cold and calculating. "I knew you'd come."

Varun stepped forward. "Ronnie, it's over. We have enough evidence to link you and Raj to these crimes. Surrender now, and it might go easier for you."

Ronnie laughed darkly. "You think you can just walk in here and take me down? You're more naive than I thought."

Varun signaled to his team to be ready for action. "Everyone, be careful," he whispered to the group. "Stick to the plan."

Varun's team captured Ronnie and his gang from behind.

Amidst the chaos, Rohan managed to reach Ronnie's computer, quickly downloading crucial evidence and deleting the pictures.

Myra, Aashi, and Eeshan watched anxiously, ready to jump in if needed. They knew this was their chance to end everything. After a lot of struggle, Varun secured Ronnie and his gang, ensuring they couldn't escape.

"It's over, Ronnie," Varun said firmly. "You'll pay for your crimes now."

As the police escorted Ronnie and his men out, the group breathed a collective sigh of relief. The nightmare that had haunted them for so long was finally over.

Myra hugged Rohan tightly, tears of relief streaming down her face. "Thank you. All of you. I couldn't have done this without you."

Eeshan, Aashi, and Varun joined the hug.

As they walked out of the warehouse, Rohan took Myra's hand and squeezed it gently. She looked up at him, her eyes filled with gratitude and something more. Rohan smiled softly. "I promised you it would end today. And it did."

Myra felt a warmth spread through her, a sense of safety she hadn't felt in a long time. "You kept your promise," she whispered, leaning her head on his shoulder as they walked.

Eeshan and Aashi shared a knowing glance, happy to see their friends find some peace. Eeshan pulled Aashi close, and she rested her head on his chest. "It's finally over," Aashi said.

Eeshan kissed her forehead. "Yes, it is. Now we can move on."

As they reached the car, Rohan turned to Myra. "How about we go somewhere nice tomorrow? Just you and me. We deserve a break."

Eeshan heard the conversation and jumped in between. "Date, huh? Can it be a double date then?"

Eeshan and Aashi looked at each other, watching the expressions of Myra and Rohan, and laughed.

Myra nervously answered, "Why not? We can all hang out together."

Rohan also agreed by nodding.

"Come on, Eeshan, don't be mean. Give them their privacy and let them enjoy their date," Aashi said, scolding Eeshan.

Eeshan giggled and said, "I was just kidding, babe. Anyway, we are going somewhere else."

Aashi jumped with excitement and asked, "Where?"

Eeshan winked and said, "Patience, babe, I have planned a surprise for you."

Aashi's excitement was visible on her face.

"Okay, guys, tomorrow love will be in the air for all of us," said Eeshan.

Rohan chuckled and added, "Let's hope Eeshan's surprise date goes smoothly. He tends to overdo things."

Myra laughed softly. "I'm sure it'll be perfect. Just like tomorrow for us."

Eeshan ended with the dialogue of a famous movie, "Ja Rohan Ja Jeele Apni Zindagi," and laughed.

Rohan and Myra exchanged a shy smile, the beginning of something new and beautiful between them.

As they drove away, the sun began to set, symbolizing a new beginning for all of them. They knew they had faced darkness together and emerged stronger, ready to embrace the light and whatever the future held.

8

PERFECT MOMENTS

The next morning, everyone woke up feeling excited. Myra and Aashi were in Myra's room, going through their clothes, laughing and chatting about what to wear for their dates.

"What do you think, Myra? This dress or the skirt?" Aashi asked, holding up two options.

Myra looked at them carefully. "The dress. It's perfect for a surprise date. Plus, it brings out your eyes."

Aashi smiled. "Thanks, Myra. What about you? You need to look amazing for Rohan."

Myra blushed and held up a floral blue sundress. "I was thinking of this. It's simple but pretty."

"It's perfect," Aashi agreed. "Rohan won't be able to take his eyes off you."

Meanwhile, in Rohan's room, he and Eeshan were also getting ready. Rohan was a bit nervous, checking his reflection in the mirror over and over.

"You look fine, man," Eeshan laughed. "Relax, it's just a date."

Rohan smiled, shaking his head. "Yeah, but it's with Myra. I want it to be special."

Eeshan clapped him on the back. "It will be. Just be yourself. She already likes you for who you are."

An hour later, they all met outside, dressed to impress. Myra and Aashi looked beautiful, Myra in her blue dress and Aashi in a pink one. Rohan and Eeshan couldn't hide their admiration. Rohan, in a blue shirt, couldn't help but notice that he and Myra were unintentionally twinning.

"You two look amazing," Rohan said, his eyes on Myra.

Myra blushed. "You look pretty handsome yourself."

Eeshan teased, "Look at you two, matching outfits and all. Did you plan this?"

Rohan and Myra exchanged shy smiles, both blushing. "It's just a coincidence," Myra said softly.

"Sure it is," Aashi giggled, joining in on the fun. "You two are adorable."

Rohan took Myra's hand and squeezed it gently. "Shall we?"

Myra nodded, feeling a flutter of excitement. They split into two groups, heading to their respective date locations. Rohan led Myra to a cozy café nestled in a quiet corner of the city. The café was decorated with fairy lights and flowers, creating a romantic ambiance.

"This place is beautiful," Myra said, her eyes sparkling.

"I'm glad you like it," Rohan replied, pulling out a chair for her. "I wanted today to be special."

They ordered coffee and pastries, and as they chatted, the conversation flowed easily. They laughed, shared stories, and discovered new things about each other. Rohan found himself captivated by Myra's laughter and the way her eyes lit up when she talked about something she loved.

As they finished their meal, Rohan reached across the table, taking Myra's hand in his. "I've had such a great time today. I'm really glad we did this."

"Me too," Myra replied, squeezing his hand. "It's been perfect."

Rohan smiled, his eyes warm. "Would you like to take a walk with me in this peaceful weather? Let's go to Lodhi Garden, what do you say?"

Myra nodded. "I'd love that."

Meanwhile, Eeshan had taken Aashi to a beautiful garden by the lake. He had set up a picnic under a large tree, complete with a blanket, cushions, and a basket filled with her favorite foods.

"A picnic? This is amazing!" Aashi exclaimed, her eyes wide with delight.

Eeshan grinned. "I wanted to do something different. I'm glad you like it."

They settled down, enjoying the delicious food and the serene surroundings. Eeshan played soft music on his phone, adding to the romantic atmosphere. As they talked, they found themselves opening up about their dreams and fears, growing closer with every word.

"I've never done anything like this before," Aashi admitted, looking out at the lake. "It's so peaceful."

Eeshan nodded. "I wanted to create a special memory for us. Something we can look back on and smile."

Aashi leaned in, resting her head on his shoulder. "You've succeeded. This is perfect."

As the sun began to set, Eeshan stood up and held out his hand. "Would you like to dance?"

Aashi giggled. "Here? In the garden?"

Eeshan nodded, a twinkle in his eye. "Why not? It's our own little world right now."

And he played the song Tum se hi din hota hai tumse hi sham aati h tum se hi ...

Aashi took his hand, and they danced under the fading light, the moment magical and intimate. Eeshan twirled her around, their laughter mingling with the rustling leaves.

When the song ended, Aashi looked up at Eeshan, her heart full. "Thank you for this beautiful day."

Eeshan kissed her forehead and answered, "I'm just glad to see you happy."

At Lodhi Garden, Myra and Rohan walked side by side, the lush greenery and historic monuments providing a picturesque backdrop.

"Myra, do you remember the first time we met?" Rohan asked.

Myra laughed softly. "Of course. It was at Eeshan's birthday party. You accidentally spilled juice on my dress."

Rohan chuckled. "I was so embarrassed. But you were so kind about it, made me feel less like an idiot."

"I remember thinking you were sweet for apologizing so much," Myra said, looking at him with a smile.

"What's your favorite flower?" Rohan asked, bending down to gently touch a petal.

"Lilies," Myra replied.

Rohan nodded. "I'll remember that."

Myra smiled. "What about you? Do you have a favorite flower?"

Rohan thought for a moment. "I think I like roses. They're classic and timeless. Plus, they smell great."

They continued walking, the peaceful atmosphere making them feel at ease. Rohan noticed a small pond ahead and led Myra towards it.

"Look at the ducks," Myra said, pointing to a pair swimming together.

"They look so cute," Rohan observed.

"This has been really nice," Myra said, leaning her head on Rohan's shoulder.

"It has," Rohan agreed. "I'm glad we did this."

Their moment was interrupted by the ring of Rohan's phone. He glanced at the screen and saw Eeshan's name.

"Hey, how's it going?" Rohan answered.

"Great! We're just finishing up. How about you guys?" Eeshan asked.

"Same here. We're just walking in the garden," Rohan replied.

"Sounds nice. We'll see you at home then?"

"Yeah, see you soon," Rohan said.

As Rohan ended the call, he turned to Myra. "Eeshan and Aashi are heading back. Shall we?"

Myra nodded. "Yes, let's go."

They walked back to the car, their hands still playing with each other's.

As they drove back, the connection between them felt stronger than ever. The evening had been filled with laughter, shared memories, and the promise of something more.

Back at home, Eeshan and Aashi were already there, waiting for them with smiles.

"How was the walk?" Aashi asked, her eyes twinkling.

"Beautiful," Myra replied, glancing at Rohan. "Just perfect."

Eeshan winked at Rohan. "Looks like someone had a great time."

Rohan smiled, not denying it. "Yeah, it was amazing."

Rohan asked, "What about you guys? How was the surprise, Aashi?"

Aashi's face lit up. "It was wonderful! Eeshan set up a picnic by the lake with all my favorite foods. It was so thoughtful."

Eeshan grinned. "I wanted it to be special." Myra nodded. "That sounds lovely. You guys really went all out."

Eeshan laughed. "Well, we all deserved a nice day after everything we've been through."

Eeshan looked at the clock. "It's getting late. We should probably call it a night."

Everyone agreed, standing up and exchanging hugs and goodnights.

As Rohan and Eeshan headed to their room, and Myra and Aashi to theirs, the atmosphere was filled with love and excitement.

In their room, Aashi and Myra sat on the bed, still buzzing with excitement.

"That was such a beautiful date," Aashi said, hugging a pillow. "Eeshan really knows how to make me feel special."

Myra smiled, remembering her own moments with Rohan. "I

know what you mean. Rohan was so sweet and thoughtful today."

Aashi leaned closer. "You two looked so cute together, especially in those matching outfits."

Myra blushed. "I was so surprised when I saw he was wearing blue too. It felt...nice." Aashi giggled. "I think it's a sign. You both looked perfect."

Meanwhile, in the other room "Man, that was an amazing date," Rohan said, leaning back against the wall . "Myra is incredible."

Eeshan nodded, grinning. "I could tell. You both seemed so happy. And those matching outfits? Classic."

Rohan laughed. "Yeah, that was a funny coincidence. But it made the day even better."

Eeshan sighed . "Today was great for all of us. I think we're all moving in the right direction."

Rohan smiled, feeling hopeful. "Definitely. I can't wait to see what happens next."

As they drifted off to sleep, their thoughts were filled with the possibilities of tomorrow, and the exciting journey ahead.

9

THE MORNING SURPRISE

Myra and Aashi woke up to the delicious aroma of breakfast wafting through the house. As they made their way to the living room, they were greeted by a delightful sight: a beautifully decorated table filled with a variety of breakfast dishes—brownies, pancakes, omelets, and coffee. There were beautiful flowers and cheerful notes:
- *"You make my heart melt like butter on a hot pancake."*
- *"To the love of my life: I hope this breakfast makes you smile."*

"Wow, this is amazing!" Aashi exclaimed, her eyes wide with surprise.

Myra couldn't help but smile. "Looks like the boys have outdone themselves."

Rohan and Eeshan stood by the kitchen, their faces beaming with pride despite the flour and batter covering their clothes.

"Good morning, ladies," Rohan greeted, pulling out chairs for them. "We thought we'd surprise you with breakfast."

Eeshan grinned. "We might not be the best cooks, but we tried our best."

Myra and Aashi exchanged glances and giggled, noticing the chaotic state of the kitchen. "It looks like you had quite an adventure," Myra teased.

"Oh, you have no idea," Rohan laughed. "We burned the first batch of pancakes, and the eggs... well, let's just say we had a few mishaps."

"But it was worth it," Eeshan added, smiling at Aashi. "We wanted to do something special for you both."

They all sat down together, enjoying the breakfast feast. The food, despite the boys' limited cooking skills, tasted delicious because it was made with love.

As they were laughing and sharing stories about the breakfast fiasco, the doorbell rang.

"Who could that be?" Myra wondered aloud.

Rohan got up to answer the door, and moments later, Myra's parents walked in. They were carrying a large basket of fruits and sweets, their faces lighting up with joy at seeing their daughter.

"Mom! Dad! What a surprise!" Myra exclaimed, rushing to hug them.

"We missed you, beta," her mother said, hugging her tightly. "We decided to come visit you."

Everyone greeted Myra's parents, trying to hide their surprise. They all gathered in the living room, making small talk as they settled in.

After a few minutes, Myra's father cleared his throat. "We have some good news for you, Myra."

Myra looked at her parents, curious. "What is it?"

Her mother smiled warmly. "We've found a nice Punjabi boy for you. He's from a good family, and we think he would be a perfect match for you."

The room fell silent. Myra's heart sank, and she could feel the tension rising. She glanced at Rohan, whose face had turned serious.

"But, Mom, Dad... I'm not ready to get married yet," Myra said, trying to keep her voice steady.

Her father frowned slightly. "We understand, beta, but you're not getting any younger. It's time to think about your future."

Eeshan and Aashi exchanged worried looks, sensing the growing unease.

"Uncle, Aunty," Eeshan began, trying to ease the tension. "We're all very supportive of Myra's decisions. She's been doing so well here, and we're all really proud of her."

Rohan, unable to remain silent, added, "With all due respect, sir, Myra has her own dreams and aspirations. It's important that she follows her heart."

Myra's parents looked at each other, a mix of confusion and concern on their faces. They were clearly taken aback by the strong reactions from Myra's friends.

Her mother sighed. "We just want what's best for you, Myra. We thought this boy would be a good match."

Myra took a deep breath, gathering her courage. "I know you have my best interests at heart, and I appreciate it. But I need more time. I want to make my own choices about my life and my future."

Her father looked at her intently, then nodded slowly. "We understand, Myra. We don't want to pressure you. Just promise us you'll think about it."

Myra smiled, relieved. "I promise, Dad. I'll think about it."

Myra's parents were there to stay with her for a few days, so everyone decided to go back to their homes to give Myra space with her parents and clear out things.

Eeshan and Aashi, sensing the tension, stood up.

"We should get going," Aashi said softly. "Thanks for breakfast, guys."

Rohan, catching Myra's eye, gave her a reassuring nod. "We'll talk later."

"We'll see you soon," Aashi promised, hugging Myra tightly.

Eeshan nodded, shaking hands with Myra. "Take care, we are just a call away."

"When you love someone deeply, you find the strength to overcome any obstacle"

After they left, Myra and her parents sat down in the living room. Her parents began talking about the boy they had chosen, but Myra's mind was elsewhere, thinking about Rohan and the future she wanted for herself.

Later that evening, after her parents had gone to bed, Myra texted Rohan.

Myra:Hey, sorry about today. My parents are staying for a few days, and things are a bit complicated.

Rohan:It's okay. I understand. How are you holding up?

Myra:It's hard. They're so excited about this boy, but I don't feel the same way. I just wish they could see things from my perspective.

Rohan:So, are you considering their choice?

Myra:What? No! I just need time to figure out how to talk to them about it.

Rohan:Oh, I thought maybe you were having second thoughts about us.

Myra:Second thoughts? Rohan, that's not what I meant at all. I'm just trying to handle my parents without hurting them.

Rohan:Sorry, I misunderstood. It's just, today was a lot, and I guess I got worried.

Myra:I get it. It's been overwhelming for all of us. Just know that I care about you, Rohan.

Rohan: I care about you too, Myra. We'll figure this out together.

Myra: Thanks, Rohan. Your support means a lot to me.

Rohan : Anytime. We'll talk more tomorrow, okay? Try to get some rest.

Myra: Okay. Goodnight, Rohan.

Rohan: Goodnight, Myra.

10

TENSION RISES

The next morning, Myra sat with her parents at the breakfast table, trying to gather the courage to talk about her own dreams.

"Mom, Dad, I understand you want the best for me, but I need to follow my own path," Myra said, trying to sound calm and gentle.

Her mother looked worried. "We just want you to be safe and happy. Marriage can help with that."

Her father nodded. "This boy is from a good family, Myra. He can take care of you."

"But I have my own dreams and goals," Myra replied. "I want to focus on my career and figure out my life before I think about marriage."

Myra, do you have someone in your life? Is that why you're denying all the marriage proposals we've brought you?" her father asked, his eyes narrowing with suspicion.

Myra's heart raced, and she felt a lump in her throat. "No, Dad, it's not like that," she said, trying to sound convincing. "I just want to focus on my career right now."

Her father looked unconvinced. "Are you sure? Because it seems like there's more to this than you're telling us."

Myra took a deep breath, trying to steady her nerves. "I promise, Dad. There's no one else. I just need some time to figure out my own path."

Her mother's eyes softened slightly, but her father remained suspicious .

"Alright ! But we're not saying you have to give up your dreams," her father said. "But having a stable relationship can help you achieve them, and you know people in the neighborhood will start talking if we don't get you married at the right age."

Meanwhile, Rohan was on a conference call with Aashi and Eeshan, talking to them about his worries.

"I feel like we're drifting apart, guys. I haven't even proposed to her yet, and I don't know if she will stick with me or if she feels the same way. We were still figuring things out and getting to know each other more, but her parents are pushing her so hard," Rohan said.

Eeshan looked thoughtful. "Give her some space, but maybe do something to show you're there for her and trust her. A small gesture can go a long way."

"I'm worried about Myra. She's under so much pressure," Aashi said, frowning.

Rohan nodded. "You're right. I need to show her that I'm here, no matter what."

Aashi sighed. "I just hope everything works out. You guys deserve to be happy."

Eeshan added, "Just be patient, Rohan. Myra's in a tough spot. Maybe you should have an honest talk with her about where you both stand and what you want for the future. It might help clear things up."

Rohan took a deep breath. "You're right. I'll talk to her and see if we can figure things out together. Thanks, guys. I needed this."

Eeshan smiled. "Anytime, man. We're here for you."

Aashi nodded in agreement. "Keep us posted. We're rooting for you both."

At Myra's house, while she was trying to convince her parents, the bell rang.

Myra's parents exchanged glances, then her father went to answer the door. Moments later, he returned with a young man and his parents.

"Myra, this is Rahul and his family," her father said, introducing them.

Myra forced a polite smile. "Nice to meet you all."

Rahul's mother smiled warmly. "We've heard so much about you, Myra. We're delighted to finally meet you."

Myra's heart sank. "Why did Dad call them now? This is the worst timing. What am I going to tell Rohan?" she thought to herself.

There was an awkward silence in the room.

Rahul's dad cleared his throat and said, "We were just nearby to meet our daughter when you called, so we thought of visiting and meeting Myra once."

"We are glad you came," said Myra's dad, thanking them.

As Myra's parents and Rahul's family sat in the living room, the atmosphere was polite but tense. Tea and snacks were laid out on the table, and the conversation began.

"Myra, we've heard you're quite talented," Rahul's mother started, smiling warmly. "Your father mentioned you've been doing exceptionally well in your studies."

Myra forced a polite smile. "Yes, Auntie. I've been focusing a lot on my career."

"So, Myra," Rahul said, trying to make a connection, "What are your interests outside of your career?"

Myra hesitated, feeling the weight of the situation. "I enjoy reading and painting in my free time. It helps me relax."

"That's wonderful," Rahul's mother said. "It's important to have hobbies. Rahul, you should tell Myra about your interests."

Rahul smiled. "I enjoy playing tennis and traveling. Maybe one day we could explore some new places together."

Myra forced another smile, feeling increasingly uncomfortable. "That sounds nice."

Sensing the tension, her father quickly added, "We think you two would make a great match. Both of you have similar values and ambitions."

Myra's mother nodded in agreement. "It's important to find common ground."

Rahul's father raised his teacup in a toast. "To new beginnings and potential partnerships."

Everyone echoed the sentiment, though Myra's smile felt increasingly strained.

As they wrapped up their visit, Rahul's mother turned to Myra one last time. "It was lovely meeting you, dear. We look forward to seeing more of you."

Myra nodded politely. "Thank you, Auntie. It was nice meeting all of you . "

After they left, Myra, disappointed, asked her dad, "Why did you call them? I was not even ready yet."

"Beta, they called us and asked. We could not say no," answered her dad.

While having the conversation with her dad, her phone rang. She went to her room to answer the call as it was Rohan.

"Hey, how are you keeping up? Everything fine at the house?" asked Rohan.

"Not exactly. I want to meet and tell you something. Is there any way we could meet?" asked Myra.

"I was about to ask the same thing," said Rohan.

"Let's meet at the coffee shop near my house," said Myra.

"Done," said Rohan.

That evening, Myra sneaked out to meet Rohan at the coffee shop.

"I miss you, Myra. We need to figure this out together," Rohan said, his eyes filled with concern.

"I know. But it's so hard with my parents around. They don't understand," Myra replied.

Rohan held her hand. "We'll get through this. I'm here for you, no matter what."

Suddenly, Myra's phone buzzed. It was her father. "Where are you?" his text read.

"Rohan, I think my dad found out," said Myra.

"I think you should go home," said Rohan.

"But I need to tell you something before I leave," said Myra.

"What is it? Did something happen?" asked Rohan.

"Yes, Rahul, the boy my dad was talking about, he and his parents came to meet me in the afternoon," said Myra.

Rohan looked tense. He tried to handle his emotions and answered, "Okay, what did they say?"

"Nothing, just normal talks," answered Myra. "They were there for just 30 minutes. I did not directly talk to the guy," clarified Myra.

Rohan, putting his hand on Myra's, said, "I trust you, babe. Don't worry about me. I am always here."

Myra, in tears, said, "Thank you for being there and believing in us."

Rohan smiled gently. "We'll get through this, Myra. We'll find a way to make our dreams come true together. Just take it one step at a time."

Myra nodded, feeling a bit more hopeful. "I know we will. Thank you for understanding."

They embraced, holding onto each other tightly, knowing they had a long journey ahead but feeling strengthened by their love and commitment.

"I should get going before my parents worry more," Myra said softly, pulling back.

Rohan nodded, his eyes full of support and concern. "Text me when you get home safely. We'll figure this out, together."

"I will," Myra promised, squeezing his hand one last time before turning to leave.

As she walked back home, Myra felt a mixture of anxiety and nervousness. She took a deep breath and stepped inside. Her parents were waiting in the living room, their expressions a mix of concern and impatience.

"Where were you, Myra?" her father asked sharply, noticing her hesitance.

"I went to meet Rohan," Myra said, steeling herself for their reaction. "I needed to talk to him about us."

Her mother's eyes widened with surprise. "Rohan? You mean that boy you've been spending so much time with?"

"Yes, Mom," Myra replied, trying to keep her voice steady.

"Is he the reason you are behaving distant with us these days and not agreeing to marriage?" her mother asked.

"I don't know, Mom. Maybe I like him, but we are still figuring things out before taking some big step," said Myra.

Her father lashed out. "So this is what you've been hiding from us? You're wasting time on some boy when you should be thinking about your future and our family's reputation!"

"Dad, it's not like that," Myra protested, tears welling up in her eyes. "Rohan supports my dreams. He understands what I want in life."

Her mother's face turned stern. "Myra, we're trying to find a good match for you, someone who can provide stability and security. What can this Rohan offer you?"

"He offers me understanding and support, Mom. Isn't that important too?" Myra pleaded.

Her father's voice was cold. "Understanding and support won't put food on the table or ensure a secure future. You're being foolish, Myra."

"I'm not being foolish!" Myra shouted, her emotions boiling

over. "I have the right to choose my own path and who I want to be with. I'm not a child anymore."

Her father's face turned red with fury. "You lied to us this morning, Myra. You said there was no one else! How could you deceive us like this?"

Myra felt a wave of guilt wash over her. "Dad, I'm sorry. I didn't want you to find out about Rohan like this. I was scared of your reaction."

"Scared of our reaction? We are your parents, Myra! We deserve to know the truth. You've made a fool out of us!" her father shouted.

Her mother's voice trembled with a mix of anger and sorrow. "Myra, we're only trying to protect you. Why couldn't you trust us enough to tell the truth?"

Myra's eyes filled with tears. "Because I knew you wouldn't understand. Rohan is important to me, and I didn't want to lose him."

There was a tense silence in the room as her parents stared at her, their expressions a mix of anger and disappointment.

Finally, her father spoke again, his voice steely and unforgiving. "If you insist on seeing this boy, Myra, you will have to make a choice. It's either your family or Rohan. We will not tolerate this disrespect any longer."

Myra felt as if the ground had been pulled out from under her. "Dad, please don't make me choose. I love you and Mom, but I also care deeply for Rohan. Can't you try to understand?"

Her father's expression hardened. "We've made our position clear. You need to decide where your priorities lie."

Her mother's eyes filled with tears, but she remained silent, standing by her husband's ultimatum.

Feeling more isolated than ever, Myra turned and walked slowly to her room, her heart heavy with the burden of their ultimatum.

As she sat on her bed, her phone buzzed with a message from Rohan: "Did you get home safe , is everything okay at home ?"

Myra replied, "Yes. It was tough. They know about us and they're furious. They told me to choose between you and them."

Rohan's response was immediate: "I'm so sorry, Myra. We'll figure this out together. I'm here for you."

Myra typed back, "I need some time to think. Things are really complicated right now."

Rohan replied, "Take all the time you need. I'm not going anywhere."

Myra put her phone down and took a deep breath. As she lay down to sleep, she reminded herself that her dreams were worth fighting for, no matter how difficult the path might be.

11

A BIRTHDAY SURPRISE

Myra woke up feeling the weight of her father's ultimatum from the previous day. Lost in her thoughts, she didn't realize what day it was until she walked into the living room. Her eyes widened in surprise as she saw the house beautifully decorated with balloons, streamers, and a big banner that read, "Happy Birthday, Myra!"

"Happy Birthday, beta!" her parents wished, smiling warmly.

Myra's heart swelled with emotion. "Mom, Dad, you remembered!"

"Of course we did," her mother said, hugging her tightly. "We wanted to make your day special."

"We know you've been stressed lately," her father added. "But today is about celebrating you."

Myra felt a lump in her throat. "Thank you so much. This means a lot to me."

"We have another surprise for you," said her mom.

"What is it?" asked Myra in excitement.

Myra's mom handed her a box and asked her to open it. Myra opened the box quickly, like a kid.

Her mom laughed. "You are still the same — no patience when it comes to opening gifts, always excited for surprises."

"Of course, Mom. I love gifts and surprises!" said Myra.

"Beta, do you like the gift?" asked her dad.

Inside the box was a pendant with Myra's initial, M, on it.

"I love it! I've always wanted a pendant like this. You remembered!" Myra said, wearing the pendant and smiling.

After enjoying a hearty breakfast with her parents, Myra decided it was the right time to talk to them about Rohan.

"Mom, Dad, there's something important I need to ask you," Myra began hesitantly.

Her parents looked at her expectantly. "What is it, Myra?"

"I want you to meet Rohan once," Myra said, trying to keep her voice steady. "I respect your decision, but I want you to trust my choice and give him a chance."

Her mother's eyes softened. "We just want you to be happy, Myra."

Her father sighed deeply. "We just worry about you, beta. We don't want you to struggle."

"I understand that, Dad. But sometimes, the best way to learn and grow is to face challenges on my own terms," Myra said.

Her father looked at her intently. "We'll respect your decision, Myra. Just promise us you'll be careful and think things through."

Myra nodded, feeling a mix of relief and anxiety. "I promise, Dad."

"Does that mean you'll give us a chance?" asked Myra.

"Yes, for your happiness, and we trust your choice," said her dad, smiling.

Myra's eyes filled with tears. "Thank you, Dad. That means so much to me."

Her mother nodded. "We love you, Myra. Just promise to keep us involved in your life. We want to share in your journey."

"I promise, Mom," Myra said, hugging her parents tightly.

Myra quickly ran to text Rohan the good news.

Myra : Hey, I have news.
Rohan : What is it?
Myra : Guess.
Rohan : Come on, Myra, spill it. Stop with the suspense.
Myra : Umm, not like this. Let's meet. And I think you're forgetting something.
Rohan : Forgetting what?
Myra : Nothing, we'll meet in the evening.
Rohan : Okay, I'll pick you up at 6.

In the evening, Myra chose a dress that was both elegant and simple, reflecting her natural beauty and grace. She wore a knee-length, light blue chiffon dress that flowed gently with her movements. The dress had a delicate lace overlay on the body, adding a touch of sophistication. It featured a V-neckline and short, fluttery sleeves that gave it a romantic feel.

She paired the dress with silver sandals that had a small heel, enough to add a bit of height but still comfortable for walking. Her accessories were minimal but meaningful: a pair of pearl earrings, a thin silver bracelet, and the new pendant her parents had gifted her that morning, which added a personal touch to her ensemble.

Myra's hair was styled in loose waves, cascading down her shoulders, and she wore light makeup that highlighted her natural features, with a soft pink lipstick and a hint of blush. As she stepped out to meet Rohan, Aashi, and Eeshan, she felt a mix of excitement and nervousness, her outfit reflecting the special occasion and her hopeful spirit.

When she arrived, Aashi and Eeshan greeted her warmly, both of them grinning.

"Happy Birthday, Myra!" Aashi exclaimed, hugging her.

"You guys remembered?" Myra asked, touched.

"Of course we did," Eeshan said. "We were just waiting to surprise you."

Rohan smiled and handed her a bouquet of flowers. "Happy Birthday, Myra. You look stunning." Rohan wore a tailored navy blue suit that highlighted his broad shoulders and fit him perfectly. His shoes were classic black leather loafers, well-shined and matching the overall sophisticated ensemble. Rohan's attire, combined with his natural charm and the sincerity in his eyes, made him look every bit the perfect gentleman, ready to make the evening unforgettable for Myra.

"Thank you, Rohan," Myra said, blushing.

As they settled at the table, Rohan's eyes sparkled with anticipation. "We have a special surprise for you tonight, Myra."

"What is it?" Myra asked, her curiosity piqued.

Rohan stood up, his heart pounding, and took Myra's hand. He led her to a beautifully decorated spot with fairy lights and a small table. He got down on one knee, holding a small velvet box.

"Myra, from the moment I met you, I knew you were special. You light up my life in ways I never thought possible. Will you do me the honor of being with me forever?" I know it is going to be tough but i am here to support you i will do everything to be with you and win hearts of yours parents Rohan asked, opening the box to reveal a sparkling ring.

Tears filled Myra's eyes as she nodded. "Yes, Rohan, yes!" "You're my today and all of my tomorrows." Added Myra

Everyone cheered, and Rohan slipped the ring onto her finger. Myra felt overwhelmed with happiness.

"I have some good news too," Myra said, smiling through her tears. "My parents have agreed to meet you."

Rohan's face lit up. "Really? That's amazing!"

Aashi and Eeshan clapped and hugged them both. "This is the best birthday ever!" Myra exclaimed, feeling like all her dreams were coming true.

As they celebrated, Rohan whispered in Myra's ear, "This is just the beginning. I have so much planned for our future."

Myra smiled, feeling a mix of excitement and anticipation. "I can't wait," she replied.

As the night went on, they laughed, danced, and shared stories. The atmosphere was filled with love and joy, making it a night to remember.

12

UNEXPECTED VISITOR

The next day, Myra woke up with a flutter of excitement in her heart. It was the day Rohan was going to meet her parents for lunch. After their heartwarming conversation yesterday, Myra had high hopes that things would go well.

Myra dressed carefully, choosing a soft pink dress that her mother loved. It was a dress that signified warmth and optimism, reflecting her hopeful mood. She wore the pendant her parents had gifted her, feeling its comforting weight against her chest.

Rohan arrived promptly at noon, looking sharp and composed in a crisp white shirt and dark jeans. He carried a bouquet of flowers for Myra's mother and a box of sweets for her father.

"Ready?" Rohan asked, his eyes sparkling with anticipation.

Myra nodded, giving him a reassuring smile. "Let's do this."

When they arrived at Myra's house, her parents were waiting in the living room. The atmosphere was a mix of nervousness and anticipation. Myra's father, Mr. Arora, stood up, his expression serious but not unkind. Mrs. Arora gave Rohan a welcoming smile, though there was a hint of concern in her eyes.

"Mr. and Mrs. Arora, thank you for inviting me," Rohan began, handing the flowers and sweets to them. "These are for you."

Mrs. Arora took the flowers, her smile softening. "Thank you, Rohan. These are lovely. Please, have a seat."

They all settled around the dining table, where a delicious spread awaited them. Myra had helped her mother prepare the meal, hoping it would create a warm, familial atmosphere.

"Everything looks wonderful, Mrs. Arora," Rohan said, genuinely impressed. "You've gone to so much trouble."

Mrs. Arora smiled modestly. "It's no trouble at all, Rohan. We wanted to make sure you felt welcome."

As they ate, Rohan engaged in polite conversation, complimenting the food and sharing stories about his family and work. He spoke about his passion for architecture, his dreams, and how much Myra meant to him.

Mr. Arora listened intently, his expression gradually softening. "You seem to have a good head on your shoulders, Rohan," he said finally. "But I need to know — what are your intentions with my daughter?"

Rohan met Mr. Arora's gaze directly. "Sir, I love Myra deeply. My intention is to build a future with her, to support her dreams and to create a life filled with love and respect. I understand your concerns, and I'm here to assure you that I am committed to making her happy."

There was a moment of silence as Mr. Arora considered Rohan's words. Finally, he nodded. "I appreciate your honesty, Rohan. We want the best for Myra, and it's important to us that she's with someone who values her as much as we do."

Just as Mr. Arora was beginning to soften, there was a sudden, unexpected knock at the door. Myra looked puzzled. "Excuse me for a moment," she said, getting up to answer it.

As she opened the door, she was taken aback to see Priya standing there. Priya was a striking woman, with long dark hair cascading over her shoulders and sharp, intense eyes that seemed to hold a world of secrets. She wore a simple but elegant dress, yet her anxious demeanor overshadowed her appearance.

"Myra, I'm sorry to barge in like this, but I really need to talk to Rohan. It's urgent," Priya said, her voice trembling slightly.

Myra felt a knot form in her stomach. "Priya, this isn't a good time. Can it wait?"

Priya shook her head, her eyes pleading. "No, it can't. Please, Myra."

Seeing no other option, Myra reluctantly allowed her in. As Priya entered the dining room, all eyes turned to her, and the atmosphere instantly grew tense.

Mr. Arora's eyes narrowed. "Who is this?" he asked, his voice laced with suspicion.

Rohan stood up, his face a mix of surprise and concern. "This is Priya," he said, glancing nervously at Myra. "She's... an old friend."

Priya cleared her throat, visibly uncomfortable under the scrutinizing gaze of Myra's parents. "I'm sorry to interrupt your lunch, but I need to speak with Rohan privately."

Myra's father wasn't having it. "Whatever you need to say can be said here. We don't appreciate interruptions, especially during such an important meal."

Priya looked at Rohan, her eyes desperate. "Rohan, please..."

Rohan, sensing the urgency in her voice, nodded. "It's okay, Priya. You can speak here."

Taking a deep breath, Priya gathered her courage. "I'm pregnant," she announced, her voice shaking. "And... I believe Rohan is the father."

The room fell silent. Myra's face went pale, and her mother gasped, bringing a hand to her mouth. Mr. Arora's expression hardened, his eyes filled with anger and disbelief.

Rohan immediately shook his head. "That's not true, Priya. We broke up months ago. There's no way I could be the father."

Myra felt like the ground was slipping from under her feet. She looked at Rohan, searching his eyes for any sign of deceit. "Rohan, is this true?" she asked, her voice barely above a whisper.

Rohan took Myra's hand, squeezing it tightly. "I promise you, Myra, I have nothing to do with this. Priya and I ended things a long time ago."

Mr. Arora stood up, his anger barely contained. "This is exactly what I was afraid of, Myra. You're getting involved with someone who clearly has a complicated past. How can you trust him now?"

Mrs. Arora, trying to calm the situation, placed a hand on her husband's arm. "Let's not jump to conclusions. Rohan, is there a way to prove what you're saying?"

Rohan nodded, his jaw set. "We can do a paternity test. I have nothing to hide."

Priya, tears streaming down her face, looked at Myra. "I'm sorry, Myra. I didn't want to cause trouble. I just needed to find out the truth."

Myra felt torn between the man she loved and the chaos

unfolding before her. "We'll figure this out," she said, her voice firmer now. "But right now, I need some time."

Priya's sudden appearance had cast a shadow over what was supposed to be a hopeful day. Myra couldn't believe what was happening. She had hoped for a smooth introduction, but now everything was in turmoil.

Mrs. Arora turned to Priya, her voice gentle but firm. "Priya, we understand you're going through a difficult time, but this is a lot to take in. We need to address this carefully."

Priya nodded, wiping her tears. "I know, and I'm sorry for the timing. I just didn't know what else to do."

Mr. Arora's face softened slightly as he looked at Priya. "We'll arrange for the test, Priya. But for now, it's best if you leave."

Priya looked at Rohan one last time, her eyes filled with a mix of regret and desperation. "Thank you," she whispered before leaving the house.

The room was left in an uneasy silence. Myra felt overwhelmed, her mind racing with questions and doubts. She turned to Rohan, her eyes searching for answers. "Rohan, why didn't you tell me about Priya before?"

Rohan sighed, running a hand through his hair. "Myra, it's not what it seems. Priya and I ended things a long time ago. I had no idea she would come here today, let alone with this news."

Mr. Arora, still standing, looked at Rohan sternly. "We need to clear this up as soon as possible, Rohan. My daughter deserves to know the truth."

Rohan nodded, his expression determined. "I agree, sir. I'll do whatever it takes to prove my innocence."

Mrs. Arora gently took Myra's hand. "Myra, let's sit down and talk this through. We need to understand everything."

They all moved to the living room, the tension still palpable. Myra sat next to her mother, feeling her support. Rohan sat across from them, looking resolute.

Mrs. Arora started, "Rohan, can you explain more about your relationship with Priya?"

Rohan took a deep breath. "Priya and I were together for a while, but we broke up because we realized we wanted different things. There were no hard feelings, and we haven't been in touch since then."

Mr. Arora asked, "When exactly did you break up?"

"About eight months ago," Rohan replied. "I haven't seen or spoken to her since."

Myra's voice was small. "Rohan, do you think there's any chance she's telling the truth?"

Rohan shook his head. "No, Myra. I'm certain. But we need to do the test to clear this up for everyone's peace of mind."

Mrs. Arora nodded and said , "It's important we handle this calmly and find out the truth."

Myra appreciated her mother's calm demeanor. It helped her steady her own nerves. "Thank you, Mom. I just... I don't know what to think right now."

Rohan reached out to Myra, his hand trembling slightly. "Myra, please believe me. I have nothing to hide. This came out of nowhere for me too."

Mr. Arora, still tense, sighed deeply. "We need to arrange the test as soon as possible. Until then, Rohan, I think it's best if you give Myra some space."

Rohan nodded, though he looked pained. "I understand, sir.

Myra, I'll leave for now, but please know that I'm here for you, whatever happens."

Myra felt a surge of conflicting emotions — love, doubt, fear. She looked at Rohan, tears brimming in her eyes. "Rohan, I need to process all of this. I... I don't know what to believe right now."

Rohan stood, his expression resolute yet saddened. "I'll do whatever it takes to prove my innocence, Myra. You mean everything to me." He turned to her parents. "Thank you for your time.

As Rohan walked out, Myra felt her world crumbling. The man she thought she knew was now surrounded by uncertainty.

Myra retreated to her room, the weight of the day's events pressing down on her. She sat on her bed, clutching the pendant around her neck, Doubts swirled in her mind, mixing with memories of happier times with Rohan.

As she stared out the window, she whispered to herself, "How could everything change so quickly?"

For the rest of the day, Myra remained in her room, lost in thought. She replayed the events over and over, hoping for some clarity. But all she felt was a growing sense of unease and a desperate need for the truth.

13

TWISTS OF FATE

That night, after everyone had left and the house was quiet, Myra lay in bed, her mind a whirlwind of thoughts. She tossed and turned, unable to find peace. Finally, she grabbed her phone and called Aashi.

"Aashi, I can't sleep," Myra said, her voice trembling.

"What's wrong, Myra?" Aashi asked, concern lacing her voice.

"It's everything... Priya, the baby... I don't know what to think," Myra admitted, tears streaming down her face.

"What do you mean?" Aashi pressed, her tone serious.

"I mean, Priya showed up and claimed Rohan is the father of her baby," Myra said, her voice breaking.

There was a stunned silence on the other end of the line. Then Aashi spoke, her voice filled with shock. "What? Are you serious?"

"Yes, I'm serious. She just barged in and dropped this bombshell in front of my parents," Myra said, wiping her tears.

"Oh my God, Myra. That's insane. What did Rohan say?" Aashi asked, her voice rising with anxiety.

"He denied it. He said it's not possible, but I don't know what to believe. I feel like my world is falling apart," Myra confessed.

"Have you talked to him since then?" Aashi asked.

"No, I couldn't. I just needed some time to think," Myra replied.

"You need to talk to him, Myra. This is too big to just leave hanging. But first, let's get Eeshan on the line. He might have some insight," Aashi suggested.

A few moments later, Eeshan's voice joined the conversation. "Hey, what's going on? Aashi said there's some big drama happening."

Myra took a deep breath and recounted the evening's events. As she spoke, Eeshan listened quietly.

"Wow, that's heavy," Eeshan said finally. "I had no idea it was this serious."

"Did you know anything about Priya still being in the picture?" Myra asked, her voice edged with suspicion.

Eeshan hesitated for a moment. "I knew she was still around, but I didn't think it was anything serious. Priya always had a hard time letting go of Rohan, but I never imagined she'd do something like this."

"Why didn't you tell me?" Myra asked, feeling a mix of hurt and anger.

"I didn't want to stir up unnecessary drama, especially since Rohan seemed committed to you," Eeshan explained. "But I should have said something. I'm sorry, Myra."

"This is a mess," Myra said, rubbing her temples. "I don't know what to do."

"We'll get through this together," Aashi said firmly. "First, you need to talk to Rohan and get his side of the story. Do not overthink or jump to any assumptions. I know it's tough, but have patience, babe. We are here for you."

Eeshan nodded in agreement. "Yes, we will sort this out. Don't worry."

The next morning, Myra felt a knot in her stomach as she texted Rohan.

Myra : Hey

Rohan : Hey, are you okay ?

Myra: Not really. I don't know what to believe. I feel so anxious.

Rohan: Stay calm. I am here. Trust me, I have not done anything. It's all a misunderstanding. I will prove it.

Myra: When are you going for the tests?

Rohan: Just getting ready. About to leave.

Myra: All the best. Update me.

Rohan: For sure. Bye, take care.

Myra: Bye

Myra put her phone down, trying to steady her breathing. She spent the morning pacing her room, unable to focus on anything else. Finally, Aashi called her.

"Hey, how are you holding up?" Aashi asked.

"Barely," Myra admitted. "I can't stop thinking about what Priya said."

"Let's meet for coffee," Aashi suggested. "You need to get out of the house and clear your mind."

Myra agreed and met Aashi at their favorite café. As they sipped their drinks, Aashi tried to distract her with light-hearted conversation, but it was clear Myra's mind was elsewhere.

"I just don't understand why Priya would lie about something like this," Myra said finally. "What does she have to gain?"

"Maybe she's desperate," Aashi said. "Or maybe there's something else going on that we don't know about."

Just then, Myra's phone buzzed with a message from Eeshan.

Eeshan: Hey, I've been doing some thinking. Can we all meet up tonight? There's something I need to tell you both.

Myra: Sure. We are at our favorite café. Can you come?

Eeshan: Okay! Will reach there in 10 minutes.

Myra: See you then.

"What did Eeshan say?" Aashi asked.

"He wants to meet. He's coming here in 10 minutes. He says there's something he needs to tell us," Myra replied, feeling a mixture of curiosity and dread.

Ten minutes later, Eeshan arrived at the café. They sat down, sipping coffee, and Eeshan took a deep breath. "I've been doing some thinking about this whole situation with Priya. There's something you should know."

"What is it?" Myra asked, her heart pounding.

"After Rohan and Priya broke up, Priya was really struggling," Eeshan began. "She made some bad choices, got involved with some questionable people. There's a chance that the father of her baby could be someone else from that time."

Myra's eyes widened. "Why didn't you tell us this earlier?"

"I didn't want to spread rumors or cause unnecessary drama,"

Eeshan explained. "But now, with everything that's happened, I think it's important you know the full picture."

"This changes everything," Aashi said, looking at Myra. "If there's a chance the baby isn't Rohan's, then we need to find out for sure."

"That's why I suggested the paternity test," Eeshan said. "It's the only way to get to the truth."

Myra nodded, feeling a mix of hope and fear. "I just want this nightmare to be over."

Meanwhile, at the hospital, as Rohan and Priya arrived for the paternity test, the atmosphere was tense. Rohan's mind was racing with thoughts of Myra and the unexpected chaos Priya had brought into their lives.

Priya, on the other hand, seemed anxious but determined. Her long dark hair was pulled back into a neat ponytail, and she wore a simple dress that highlighted her tense demeanor. As they approached the reception desk, Rohan could feel the weight of the situation pressing down on him.

"We're here for a paternity test," Rohan said to the receptionist, trying to keep his voice steady.

The receptionist nodded and handed them some forms to fill out. "Please fill these out and take a seat. The doctor will call you shortly."

As they sat down, Priya turned to Rohan. "Thank you for coming, Rohan. I know this isn't easy for you."

Rohan didn't meet her gaze. "I'm only here to clear my name and prove to Myra that this has nothing to do with me."

Priya sighed, her eyes showing a hint of regret. "I never wanted to cause this much trouble. I just needed to know the truth."

Before Rohan could respond, a nurse called their names. "Mr. Rohan and Ms. Priya, the doctor is ready for you."

They followed the nurse into a small examination room where a doctor greeted them. "Good morning. We'll be collecting samples for the paternity test today. This process is straightforward and will only take a few minutes."

The doctor took Rohan's sample first, swabbing the inside of his cheek. Rohan sat still, trying to stay calm. After the doctor finished, Priya's sample was taken in the same manner.

Once the samples were collected, the doctor gave them a reassuring smile. "We'll have the results in a few days. We'll contact you once they're ready."

As they left the hospital, Priya stopped Rohan. "Rohan, I know you're angry, but I want you to know that whatever happens, I never intended to hurt you or Myra."

Rohan looked at her, his eyes cold. "Priya, this isn't just about us anymore. You've brought Myra and her family into this mess. I hope for everyone's sake that the truth comes out soon."

Priya nodded, tears welling up in her eyes. "I'm sorry, Rohan. Truly."

Rohan didn't respond. He walked away, leaving Priya standing alone, her shoulders slumped in despair.

Back at the café, Eeshan, Myra, and Aashi sat in silence, processing everything Eeshan had revealed. Myra's mind was still a whirlwind, but for the first time, she felt a glimmer of hope. Maybe there was a way out of this nightmare after all.

"We'll get through this," Aashi repeated, squeezing Myra's hand. "No matter what."

Just then Rohan's name lit up on Myra's phone screen, making her heart skip a beat. With a deep breath, she answered the call.

"Hello?" she said, her voice trembling.

"Hey, Myra," Rohan replied, his voice steady but clearly anxious. "I just gave the samples for the paternity test. The results will take a few days."

Myra took a deep breath, trying to steady her racing heart. "Thank you for letting me know, Rohan."

"I know this is a lot to handle," Rohan said, his tone softening. "But I want you to know that I'm here for you, and I'll do whatever it takes to prove that I'm not the father of Priya's baby."

Myra felt a surge of emotion, torn between hope and fear. "I want to believe you, Rohan. This whole situation is just so overwhelming."

"I understand," Rohan said. "I wish there was something more I could do right now. We just have to wait for the results."

"Yeah," Myra replied, her voice barely above a whisper. "I guess we do."

"Can we meet tomorrow?" Rohan asked hesitantly. "I think it would help if we talked more about this face-to-face."

Myra hesitated, feeling overwhelmed by the situation. "I don't think I can, Rohan. I need some time to process all of this. I hope you understand."

Rohan sighed, a mix of disappointment and understanding in his voice. "I get it, Myra. Take all the time you need. Just know that I'm here whenever you're ready to talk."

"Thanks, Rohan," Myra replied, her voice soft. "I'll let you know."

After ending the call, Myra felt a wave of exhaustion wash over her. She looked at Aashi and Eeshan, who had been watching her with concern.

"He gave the samples today," Myra explained. "The results will take a few days. He wanted to meet tomorrow, but I told him I need more time."

Aashi reached out and hugged her tightly. "You did the right thing, Myra. Take all the time you need to sort through your feelings."

Eeshan nodded in agreement. "We're here for you, Myra. No matter what happens, we'll face it together."

When Myra arrived home, she found a note on the kitchen counter. It was from her parents, who had to leave for a relative's place due to an emergency and her phone was not reachable .Myra felt more anxious and alone.

She immediately called Aashi. "Aashi, I just got home and saw the note from my parents. They had to leave for an emergency and I'm here by myself. Can you come over? I really don't want to be alone right now."

Aashi's voice was full of concern. "Of course, Myra. I'll be there as soon as I can. Just hang tight. I'm on my way."

Within a short while, Aashi arrived at Myra's house, carrying a bag with some snacks and comfort items. She immediately set about making the place feel more welcoming, chatting with Myra to help ease her nerves.

"It's going to be okay," Aashi said as she unpacked the snacks and settled on the couch. "We'll get through this together."

Myra nodded, feeling a mix of relief and gratitude. "Thank you, Aashi. I don't know what I'd do without you."

Aashi smiled warmly. "You don't have to worry about that. I'm here for you. Let's try to relax and take things one step at a time."

The evening passed slowly but peacefully with Aashi's comforting presence. They watched light-hearted movies and chatted about everything and nothing, trying to push the worries of the day aside. Myra appreciated the distraction, though her mind often wandered back to the looming uncertainty of the test results.

As the night grew late, they finally decided to head to bed.

14

FACING THE TRUTH

Myra had avoided Rohan for days, while her parents continued to express their concerns about him. Each time they inquired, she mumbled noncommittal answers, her mind elsewhere. She needed to process the whirlwind of emotions that had consumed her life since Priya's bombshell revelation.

Her parents, sensing her distress but unsure how to help, were also confused. They tried to comfort her with small gestures — her mother's home-cooked meals, her father's attempts at light-hearted conversation — but nothing seemed to break through the wall Myra had built around herself. She seemed depressed.

One morning, as she sat at the kitchen table staring blankly at her untouched breakfast, her mother gently touched her shoulder. "Myra, sweetheart, we're worried about you. Have you spoken to Rohan?"

Myra shook her head, her eyes filling with tears. "No, Mom. I just... I need some time."

Her father joined them, his expression serious. "We understand,

Myra. But avoiding him won't solve anything. You need to face this, whatever it is."

Just then, her phone buzzed with a message from Rohan.

Rohan: Myra, the test results are back.

Myra: What is it?

Rohan: It is negative. I am not the father. Can we meet?

Myra: Um, okay. Let's meet in an hour.

Rohan: Sure, I will pick you up.

Myra stared at the screen, her heart pounding. Relief washed over her, but so did a fresh wave of confusion and fear. She took a deep breath and calmed herself down. A short while later, Rohan arrived at Myra's house to pick her up.

"Myra, I've missed you," he said softly, reaching for her hand.

She took his hand, squeezing it tightly. "I've missed you too."

Myra still looked stressed, so Rohan asked, "Is everything okay? I thought you would be happy after this. Why do you look disturbed now?"

Myra hesitated before replying, "I think we should confront Priya about why she lied."

Rohan gave it a thought and nodded. "You are right. I think we should."

They drove in silence to Priya's house, each lost in their own thoughts. When they arrived, Myra felt a knot of anxiety tighten in her stomach. She glanced at Rohan, who nodded reassuringly. Together, they walked up to the door and knocked.

Priya answered, looking surprised and uneasy. "Myra, Rohan... what are you doing here?"

"We need to talk," Myra said firmly. "Can we come in?"

Priya hesitated but then stepped aside to let them enter. They sat down in her small living room, the tension palpable.

"Priya, the paternity test came back negative," Rohan began, his voice steady but intense. "I'm not the father of your baby. We need to know why you lied."

Priya's eyes filled with tears, and she looked away, clearly ashamed. "I'm sorry," she whispered. "I was scared. That night, after we broke up, I went to a club. I got drunk and... I hooked up with someone. I don't even remember who it was."

Myra's heart softened slightly, seeing the genuine remorse in Priya's eyes. "Why didn't you tell us the truth from the beginning?"

Priya wiped her tears, her voice trembling. "I thought if I said it was you, Rohan, it would be simpler. I didn't want to admit what I'd done. I was afraid... afraid of facing the reality of my actions."

Rohan sighed, the anger he'd been holding onto dissipating. "Priya, we could have helped you. You didn't have to go through this alone."

"I know," Priya said, her voice breaking. "I'm so sorry. I never meant to hurt either of you. I was just so scared and ashamed."

Myra reached out and took Priya's hand, squeezing it gently. "We understand now. But you need to be honest with yourself and with us from now on. We all make mistakes, but we can't run from them."

Priya nodded, tears streaming down her face. "Thank you for understanding. I'll do whatever it takes to make things right."

Rohan glanced at Myra, his expression softening. "Myra, I'm so sorry for everything you've been through. I never wanted to cause you pain."

Myra looked into his eyes, seeing the sincerity and love there. "I know, Rohan. This has been hard for all of us, but I still believe in us."

They left Priya's house with clarity in their minds.

As they drove back to Myra's house, Myra invited Rohan to come inside and meet her parents. Her parents greeted them warmly, their worry replaced by relief.

"Rohan, it's good to see you, and we are glad the misunderstandings got cleared," Myra's mother said, embracing him. "We've been so concerned."

"Thank you," Rohan replied, his voice sincere. "I'm sorry for all the worry and trouble."

They gathered in the living room, the atmosphere now more relaxed. Myra's father, always the practical one, spoke up. "We're just glad to have this behind us. What's important is that you both move forward."

Myra nodded, her hand still entwined with Rohan's. "We will. We've been through a lot, but it's made us stronger."

Her mother smiled warmly. "That's the spirit. And speaking of moving forward..."

Myra's father cut in, a twinkle in his eye. "We were thinking it's time to start planning for the future. I know you have just got out of trouble, but I think we should not stretch it more."

Rohan's eyes widened with joy. "I think you are right, Uncle. I want to get married to Myra, and I think it's time we take this decision."

Myra felt a surge of happiness at the thought. "Yes, I think it's time we started planning."

Myra's mom nodded and asked, "Rohan, are your parents aware?"

Rohan replied, "Yes, I have told them from the start that I like Myra. I will talk to them about getting married."

Myra's father smiled broadly. "That's great news. We should meet your parents and discuss everything."

Rohan nodded. "I'll call them today and let them know. They will be thrilled."

As the families began to discuss wedding plans, Myra felt a sense of peace and happiness she hadn't felt in a long time. The dark clouds of doubt and confusion had finally lifted, and the future looked bright and promising.

"True love isn't about avoiding storms, but about dancing together in the rain."

15

THE BIG STEP

Myra woke up with a flutter of excitement in her heart. The thought of getting married filled her with joy and anticipation. She couldn't wait to share her happiness with Rohan, so she quickly grabbed her phone and called him, momentarily forgetting that it was still quite early.

Rohan, still in a deep sleep, picked up the call. "Hello?" he mumbled, his voice thick with sleep.

Myra couldn't help but giggle. "Good morning, sleepyhead. I'm so sorry for waking you up, but I just couldn't wait to talk to you."

Rohan yawned, a smile creeping into his voice. "It's okay, Myra. Your voice is the best wake-up call. What's got you so excited this early?"

Myra's cheeks flushed as she replied, "I was just thinking about our future... our wedding. I can't believe it's actually happening."

Rohan chuckled softly. "I can't believe it either. I'm the luckiest guy in the world to have you."

Myra's heart swelled with love. "You know, your sleepy voice is really sexy," she teased playfully.

Rohan laughed, a warm, deep sound that sent shivers down Myra's spine. "Oh yeah? Well, I think your voice is pretty sexy too, especially when you're all excited like this."

"Hey, I have an idea," Myra said suddenly. "Let's tell Aashi and Eeshan about our plans. I want to see their reactions in person."

Rohan agreed, his excitement matching hers. "That sounds perfect. Let's call them and set up a meeting."

Myra switched the call to a conference call and dialed Aashi and Eeshan's numbers. After a few rings, both of them picked up.

"Hey, what's up?" Aashi's cheerful voice came through.

"Good morning!" Eeshan added, sounding curious.

"Good morning, guys," Myra began, her voice bubbling with excitement. "Rohan and I have a surprise for you, but we want to tell you in person. Can you meet us at Café Coffee Day near my house in an hour?"

Aashi's curiosity was piqued. "A surprise? Now I'm intrigued. We'll be there!"

Eeshan agreed, his tone enthusiastic. "Count me in. See you both soon."

Myra ended the call and turned her attention back to Rohan. "I can't wait to see their faces when we tell them."

Rohan laughed. "Me neither. This is going to be fun."

They spent the next hour getting ready, the anticipation building with each passing minute. When the time finally came, they made their way to Café Coffee Day, their hearts full of joy and excitement.

As they arrived at the café, they spotted Aashi and Eeshan already seated at a corner table, their expressions a mix of curiosity and excitement. Myra and Rohan exchanged a knowing glance before making their way over to join their friends.

"Hey, you two!" Aashi greeted them with a wide smile. "What's this big surprise you've been teasing us about? And what was the test result? Come on, spill the suspense!"

"Wait, wait, we'll answer everything. What's the rush?" Myra teased.

"Come on, stop this buildup and just tell us!" Eeshan said, eager for answers.

"Okay, fine," Rohan said, playing along. "First, let's clear the air. I'm not the father. The tests came back negative."

"That's amazing news! I knew it! Thank God everything is back to normal," Aashi said, clearly relieved.

"That's great, guys. So, what's the other news?" Eeshan asked, still curious.

Rohan's eyes twinkled with mischief. "So, you guys know how much Myra and I have been through lately, right? All the misunderstandings and drama?"

Aashi nodded eagerly. "Yes, we know. And we're so glad things are getting better for you two."

"Well," Myra continued, drawing out the moment, "we've decided to take a big step forward."

Eeshan raised an eyebrow. "A big step, huh? Are you moving in together or something? Like a live-in relationship?"

Myra couldn't hold it in any longer. She burst out laughing. "No, silly! We're getting married!"

Aashi's jaw dropped, and she let out a delighted squeal. "Oh my God! That's amazing! Congratulations!"

"When did this happen? I mean, when did you decide this all of a sudden?" Eeshan asked, surprised.

Myra and Rohan explained the conversation with Myra's parents to them.

Eeshan's face lit up with a wide grin. "Wow, that's incredible news! I'm so happy for you both!"

"So, have you guys set a date yet?" Aashi asked, her eyes sparkling with curiosity.

"Not yet," Myra admitted. "We wanted to talk to our families first and make sure everyone is on board."

Rohan nodded in agreement. "Yeah, I haven't talked to my parents about it yet."

"What are you waiting for, silly?" Aashi asked, surprised.

"I was thinking of talking to them today and taking Myra home to meet them. What do you think?" Rohan suggested.

"What? Really? Why didn't you tell me? I would've worn a cute kurti to impress her! I'll be meeting her for the first time, and I want to be in an ethnic outfit," Myra said, slightly panicked.

"Come on, she's modern. It doesn't matter, babe," Rohan reassured her.

"No, Myra is right. She has to make a good first impression," Aashi interrupted.

"Hmm," Eeshan nodded in agreement.

"Okay, so let's go to the mall on the way to my house. I'll buy you a kurti, you can change at the mall, and then we'll go to my house," Rohan said, making a quick plan.

"That sounds good," Myra agreed.

Aashi nodded in approval.

"Let's rush then, we have so much to do!" Myra said, suddenly feeling the time crunch.

"Aashi and Eeshan, you're coming with us! I need your help in shopping and some motivation," Myra added.

"Okay, let's go," Aashi and Eeshan agreed, ready to help.

They drove to the mall near Rohan's house, excitement buzzing in the car. As they reached the mall, Myra quickly rushed to a showroom and started looking for a kurti.

"Come on, guys, we don't have time! Aashi, come help me choose an outfit," Myra called out, scanning the racks.

"I think this pink one will look good. You should try it," Aashi suggested, handing her a kurti she had picked out.

Myra took it, kept it in her shopping bag, and continued looking for more options. She quickly grabbed a few more outfits and headed to the trial room.

After trying three outfits, Myra finally stepped out in a blue kurti paired with narrow pants. She added jhumkas to complete her look, transforming into a perfect, beautiful desi girl.

"Oh my God, I feel like I might faint. Is this pretty woman really mine?" Rohan complimented her, giving her a flirty smile.

"You look perfect, my girl. I'm sure you'll make a great impression now," Aashi said, admiring her friend.

"You look beautiful, bhabhi," Eeshan teased, making Rohan and Myra blush.

After paying the bill, they all rushed to Rohan's house.

As they drove toward Rohan's house, Myra began to feel a wave of nervousness , her mind racing with thoughts about meeting Rohan's parents for the first time.

Rohan noticed her discomfort and reached over to gently squeeze her hand. "Hey, don't worry, Myra. My parents are going to love you."

Myra gave him a small smile but couldn't shake the anxiety. "What if they don't, Rohan? What if I don't make a good first impression?"

Aashi, sitting in the back seat, leaned forward to join the conversation. "Myra, you look absolutely beautiful, and more importantly, you're an amazing person. How could anyone not love you?"

Eeshan chimed in from beside her. "Exactly. You've got nothing to worry about. Just be yourself. They'll see how incredible you are, just like we all do."

Myra sighed, feeling slightly better but still uncertain. "It's just that this is such an important meeting. I want everything to go perfectly."

Rohan glanced at her, his eyes filled with reassurance. "It will go perfectly, Myra. My mom is really easygoing and modern. She's going to appreciate how thoughtful you are, dressing up and wanting to make a good impression."

"And even if something doesn't go exactly as planned," Aashi added, "just remember that Rohan's already head over heels for you. His parents will see that, and that's what really matters."

Eeshan nodded enthusiastically. "Yeah, and if they see how happy you make Rohan, they'll be thrilled. Besides, you've got us by your side for moral support."

Myra laughed softly, feeling a warmth spread through her heart. "You guys are the best. Thanks for the pep talk. I'm feeling a little better now."

Rohan smiled, his thumb gently caressing her hand. "That's the spirit, Myra. We're in this together, and no matter what, I've got your back."

"Plus, if you start feeling nervous, just remember how amazing you looked in that blue kurti and how Rohan almost fainted," Aashi teased, making everyone laugh.

"Yeah, I did almost faint. Seriously, Myra, you're stunning," Rohan added, giving her a playful wink.

Myra's nervousness started to melt away as the car filled with laughter and lighthearted banter. Her friends' words of encouragement, along with Rohan's unwavering support, made her feel more confident. She took a deep breath, resolving to face the upcoming meeting with her best foot forward.

As they approached Rohan's house, Myra felt a mix of excitement and determination. No matter what happened, she knew she had the love and support of those closest to her, and that gave her the strength she needed to meet Rohan's parents with confidence.

16

THE MEETING

As the car neared Rohan's home, Eeshan and Aashi waved goodbye, offering Myra last-minute encouragement before heading off to their respective plans for the day. Myra watched them go, a mixture of gratitude and nervousness swirling in her chest. With a final reassuring smile from Rohan, they continued toward his house, a place that would soon hold even greater significance in her life.

The car came to a stop in front of a charming, two-story house with a neatly manicured lawn and vibrant flower beds. Myra's heart raced as she took in the picturesque scene, realizing that this was where Rohan had grown up, where countless memories had been made.

As they stepped out of the car, the front door of the house opened, and Rohan's mother appeared in the doorway. She was a graceful woman in her late forties, with kind eyes and a warm smile that immediately put Myra at ease. She wore a simple, elegant sari, and her hair was neatly pulled back into a bun.

"Rohan, Myra, welcome!" she called out, her voice full of warmth. She descended the steps to greet them, her smile widening as she took in the sight of Myra. "You must be Myra. I've heard so much about you."

Myra's nerves momentarily melted away as she returned the smile, feeling genuinely welcomed. "Yes, Aunty. It's so nice to finally meet you," she replied, her voice steadier than she expected.

Rohan's mother embraced her in a gentle hug, her touch filled with motherly affection. "I'm so happy you're here. Please, come inside."

They all followed her into the house, where the scent of freshly brewed tea and something sweet wafted through the air. The interior was just as inviting as the exterior, with soft, earth-toned furnishings and family photos adorning the walls. Myra couldn't help but feel a sense of warmth and belonging as she took in her surroundings.

In the living room, Rohan's father was seated in an armchair, reading a newspaper. He looked up as they entered and immediately stood, a broad smile spreading across his face. He was a tall man with a dignified presence, yet his eyes held the same warmth as Rohan's mother.

"Ah, you must be Myra," he said, extending his hand in greeting. "It's a pleasure to finally meet the young lady who's stolen our son's heart."

Myra blushed as she shook his hand, touched by his kind words. "Thank you, Uncle. It's an honor to meet you as well."

"Come, sit down, all of you," Rohan's mother urged, gesturing toward the comfortable sofa. "We've prepared some tea and snacks. I hope you're hungry."

As they settled into the plush seats, Rohan's mother disappeared into the kitchen, returning moments later with a tray laden with cups of steaming tea, samosas, and a plate of homemade sweets. She placed the tray on the coffee table and poured each of them a cup, her hospitality making Myra feel even more welcome.

"So, Myra," Rohan's father began as he sipped his tea, "Rohan tells us that you're quite the artist. I'd love to hear more about your work."

Myra smiled, grateful for the chance to talk about something she was passionate about. "Yes, I've always loved painting and sketching. I work mainly with watercolors and charcoal. It's a way for me to express myself and capture the beauty I see in the world."

Rohan's mother's eyes lit up with interest. "That sounds wonderful. I'd love to see some of your work sometime. Maybe we can even hang one of your paintings here in the house."

Myra felt her nerves easing with each passing moment. The conversation flowed naturally, with Rohan's parents showing genuine interest in getting to know her. They asked about her family, her hobbies, and her future plans. Myra found herself opening up more than she had expected, sharing stories and laughing at Rohan's childhood antics as recounted by his parents.

As the conversation continued, Rohan's mother glanced at her husband, a knowing look passing between them. "Myra, there's something we wanted to talk to you about," she began, her tone gentle but serious.

Myra's heart skipped a beat, the nerves returning as she wondered what they might say next. "Of course, Aunty," she replied, trying to keep her voice steady.

Rohan's father leaned forward slightly, his expression sincere. "We wanted to say that we're very happy for you and Rohan.

It's clear that you both care deeply for each other, and that means a lot to us. But marriage is a big step, and it's important that you both go into it with open eyes and open hearts."

Rohan's mother nodded in agreement. "Marriage is about more than just love—it's about trust, understanding, and compromise. There will be challenges along the way, but as long as you stand by each other and communicate openly, you'll be able to overcome anything."

Myra listened intently, absorbing their words of wisdom. She appreciated their honesty and the care with which they spoke. "Thank you for your advice, Aunty, Uncle. I promise to always do my best to support Rohan and be there for him, no matter what."

Rohan's mother reached out and gently squeezed Myra's hand, her eyes filled with warmth. "I have no doubt that you will, Myra. We're so happy to welcome you into our family."

The sincerity in her words touched Myra deeply, and she felt tears prick at the corners of her eyes. She blinked them away, smiling gratefully. "Thank you so much. It means the world to me."

Rohan, who had been quietly observing the exchange, felt a surge of pride and love for both Myra and his parents. Seeing them connect like this, seeing Myra embraced so warmly by his family, made him feel like the luckiest man in the world. He reached over and took Myra's hand in his, giving it a reassuring squeeze.

After a few more minutes of conversation, Rohan's mother suggested they take a break from talking and enjoy the snacks she had prepared. As they ate, the atmosphere lightened further, filled with laughter and easy banter. Myra felt completely at ease now, as if she had always been a part of this family.

Once they had finished eating, Rohan's mother offered to show Myra around the house, giving her a glimpse into the home where Rohan had grown up. They walked through the cozy living room, the sunlit dining area, and the quiet study filled with bookshelves. Rohan's mother shared little anecdotes about Rohan's childhood as they went along, and Myra couldn't help but smile at the stories of his mischievous antics.

As they returned to the living room, Rohan's mother paused, looking thoughtful. "Myra, there's one more thing I'd like to share with you," she said, leading her to a small alcove near the staircase. On the wall was a framed photograph of a young couple on their wedding day — Rohan's parents.

"This was taken on our wedding day," Rohan's mother explained, her voice soft with nostalgia. "We were about your age, and just as in love as you and Rohan are now. But we've learned over the years that love alone isn't enough to sustain a marriage. It's the small things — patience, kindness, and a willingness to compromise — that make all the difference."

Myra studied the photograph, taking in the youthful faces of Rohan's parents, their smiles radiant with hope and love. She felt a deep respect for the life they had built together, and for the wisdom they had gained along the way.

"I'll remember that, Aunty," Myra said quietly, her heart full of gratitude. "Thank you for sharing this with me."

Rohan's mother smiled, her eyes shining with affection. "I know you and Rohan will build a beautiful life together. And remember, we'll always be here to support you both, no matter what."

After the house tour, everyone gathered back in the living room, where the conversation turned to lighter topics — travel, hobbies, and funny family stories. Myra found herself laughing along with everyone, feeling as though she had known Rohan's family for years instead of just a few hours.

Rohan's father was particularly keen on sharing stories from his youth. "You know," he said, leaning back in his chair with a chuckle, "Rohan used to be terrified of dogs. It wasn't until he was about twelve that he finally overcame that fear. And how did it happen? Well, he made a friend who had the tiniest, most harmless puppy you could imagine."

Rohan groaned, rubbing the back of his neck. "Dad, not that story again..."

But Myra was curious, smiling as she encouraged Rohan's father to continue. "Please, Uncle, do tell!"

"Well," Rohan's father continued with a grin, "this little puppy—named Muffin, if I remember correctly—was so small that it could fit in the palm of your hand. The first time Rohan saw it, he refused to go near it. But that little pup was persistent and kept following him around. Eventually, Rohan had no choice but to pick it up. And you know what? That was it. He fell in love with the puppy and lost his fear of dogs completely. In fact, he started begging us to get one!"

Rohan laughed, shaking his head. "It's true. Muffin was adorable.

"It's true. Muffin was adorable. I couldn't resist," Rohan admitted, a smile tugging at the corners of his lips.

Myra giggled, imagining a younger Rohan being chased by a tiny puppy. "That's such a sweet story. I'm glad you got over your fear!"

Aashi, who had been sitting quietly on the side, chimed in with interest. "So did you end up getting a dog, Rohan?"

Rohan nodded, leaning back in his chair as he reminisced. "We did. A few years later, we got a Labrador named Bruno. He was the best dog—so loyal and friendly. We had him for many years."

Rohan's mother's eyes softened as she remembered. "Bruno was like a member of the family. He brought so much joy to our lives."

The conversation drifted into a discussion about pets, with each person sharing fond memories of animals they had loved. Myra felt herself relaxing even more, finding common ground with Rohan's family in these simple, heartfelt stories.

After a while, Rohan's father turned to Myra with a curious expression. "Myra, I'm curious—what are your thoughts on the kind of wedding you and Rohan would like? Have you two discussed it yet?"

Myra blushed slightly, realizing that they hadn't gone into much detail about the wedding plans. "We've talked about it a little, but we haven't made any firm decisions yet. I think we both want something that feels meaningful and true to who we are—nothing too extravagant, but something that brings together our families and closest friends."

Rohan nodded in agreement. "We want it to be a celebration of love and unity. And, of course, we'd love for both of our families to be involved in the planning."

Rohan's mother smiled warmly. "That sounds perfect. I'm sure we can work together to create a beautiful and memorable day for you both."

Rohan's father leaned back, a contented look on his face. "No matter what you decide, the most important thing is that it reflects who you are as a couple. It's your day, after all."

Myra felt a surge of affection for Rohan's parents. Their support and understanding meant the world to her. She couldn't have asked for a better family to marry into.

The evening continued with more conversation, laughter, and shared stories. Rohan's parents made Myra feel like she truly belonged, and by the time the evening drew to a close, any remaining nerves she had felt were completely gone. She knew she had made a good impression, but more importantly, she knew that she was genuinely loved and accepted by Rohan's family.

As the clock ticked closer to the time they needed to leave, Rohan's mother stood up and began to gather the empty cups and plates. "It's getting late. You two must be tired after such a long day."

Myra nodded, "Yes, it's been a wonderful day. Thank you so much for having me."

Rohan's mother placed the dishes on a tray and then turned back to Myra, her eyes filled with affection. "We're so glad you came, Myra. You've made this house feel even more like home. And remember, you're always welcome here, anytime."

As they said their goodbyes, Rohan's mother hugged Myra tightly, whispering in her ear, "You're going to be a wonderful daughter-in-law, Myra. We're so happy to have you in our lives."

Tears welled up in Myra's eyes as she hugged Rohan's mother back, her heart overflowing with gratitude and love. "Thank you, Aunty. I'm so happy to be a part of your family."

Rohan's father gave Myra a warm handshake and a smile that conveyed his approval and affection. "Take care, Myra. We'll see you again soon."

Rohan's mother handed them a small container filled with leftover sweets. "For the road," she said with a wink. "A little something to remind you of home."

As they left Rohan's house and drove back, Myra sat quietly

in the car, reflecting on the day's events. The nerves she had felt that morning seemed like a distant memory now. She felt a deep sense of peace, knowing that she was truly accepted and loved by Rohan's family.

Rohan reached over and took her hand, smiling at her in the darkness of the car. "You were amazing today, Myra. I'm so proud of you."

Myra smiled back, squeezing his hand. "I couldn't have done it without you, Rohan. I'm so grateful to have you in my life."

They drove in comfortable silence for a while, the rhythmic hum of the car and the occasional glow of streetlights creating a soothing atmosphere. Myra felt a warmth in her chest that she couldn't quite describe — a feeling of belonging, of being part of something bigger than herself.

After a few minutes, Rohan broke the silence. "You know, my parents really like you. They couldn't stop talking about how wonderful you are after you stepped out for a moment."

Myra felt her cheeks warm with a blush. "They did?"

Rohan nodded, his eyes soft as he glanced at her. "They did. They think you're perfect for me. And they're right."

Myra's heart swelled with emotion, and she leaned her head against Rohan's shoulder. "I'm so happy, Rohan. Today was more than I could have ever hoped for."

Rohan kissed the top of her head, his voice tender. "Me too, Myra. Me too."

And as they drove into the night, hand in hand, Myra felt certain that whatever the future held, it would be beautiful.

"Love is when you find someone who feels like home, not just to your heart, but to your soul, where every moment together feels like you belong."

17

PREPARATIONS BEGIN

After a few days the preparations for Myra and Rohan's wedding were in full swing. Both their homes were buzzing with activity. The quiet rooms that once held only the daily sounds of life were now filled with laughter, the rustling of clothes, the clinking of jewelry, and the excited chatter of family members.

Myra stood in front of her bedroom mirror, admiring herself in her bridal lehenga. It was a beautiful red and gold outfit, rich in color, and decorated with intricate embroidery. As she turned slowly, the heavy fabric swayed, catching the light and shining like something magical.

Myra's heart filled with happiness and a little bit of nervousness. She had dreamt about this moment for so long, but now that it was real, it felt almost surreal.

Just then, Aashi, burst into the room. Her eyes widened when she saw Myra. "Myra, you look so beautiful! You're going to look like a princess on your wedding day," Aashi said, running over to take a closer look.

Myra blushed and smiled. "Do you really think so, Aashi? I want everything to be perfect."

Aashi nodded with enthusiasm. "Absolutely! You and Rohan are like a perfect couple. He's going to be speechless when he sees you in this."

The thought of Rohan seeing her in this outfit made Myra's heart flutter. She hadn't seen Rohan since they started the wedding preparations, and she missed him terribly. They had been so busy, but they still found time to send each other loving messages throughout the day. Myra walked over to her phone and saw a new message from Rohan.

Rohan: Just finished my sherwani fitting. Can't wait to see your reaction when you see me in it. Can we skip all the preparations and just get married already?

Myra laughed softly and quickly typed back a reply.

Myra: I can't wait to see you in your sherwani either. But we have to get through all the preparations first! Don't worry, though. It'll all be worth it when we're finally together.

Rohan: As long as we're together, I'm ready for anything.

Myra's heart swelled with love as she read his words. She set her phone down and turned back to Aashi, who was grinning at her. "You two are so cute," Aashi teased. "You're going to make everyone cry at the wedding with how sweet you are."

Myra shook her head, still smiling. "I just hope I don't cry too much. I've heard crying and makeup don't mix well!"

Aashi laughed. "Don't worry, I'll be there with tissues and a makeup touch-up kit. Now, let's go find Eeshan. He's probably trying to convince the dance teacher to add some crazy move to your dance."

They left Myra's room and walked down the hallway, where

they could hear faint music coming from one of the larger rooms .

When they entered, the room was buzzing with energy. A group of people was gathered around the dance floor, where the choreographer was showing Eeshan a series of steps. Rohan wasn't there, and Myra felt a mix of relief and disappointment.

Eeshan spotted them immediately and waved them over. "Myra! Aashi! Perfect timing. We're just about to start the run-through for the sangeet dance. Myra, come and see what you think. I promise I haven't added too many crazy moves."

Myra smiled and nodded, joining the group. As she watched Eeshan and the others practice, her thoughts drifted back to Rohan. She missed him more than she wanted to admit, but she knew that the wait would make their reunion on the wedding day all the more special.

The dance practice went smoothly, with Eeshan showing off his skills and everyone laughing at his enthusiasm. The atmosphere was light and fun, and Myra found herself relaxing, even though her thoughts kept wandering back to Rohan.

As the practice wrapped up, Aashi nudged Myra gently. "You're thinking about him, aren't you?"

Myra smiled softly. "I am. I just can't wait to see him again. It feels like it's been forever." Aashi nodded understandingly. "It's only a few more days. And then, you'll have the rest of your life together."

Myra's heart fluttered at the thought. "You're right. It's just... I'm so excited and nervous at the same time."

Aashi squeezed her hand. "That's how you know it's real. Don't worry, Myra. Everything's going to be perfect."

The days leading up to the wedding were busy, but filled with excitement. Myra and Aashi spent hours at different boutiques, trying on dresses, jewelry, and selecting the perfect outfits for each wedding event. They laughed and joked, enjoying the process of finding just the right look for Myra's big day.

Meanwhile, Rohan was busy with his own preparations, trying to make sure everything was just right for the wedding. He had been working closely with his friends and family, ensuring that every detail was taken care of.

While they were trying sherwanis Rohan look a bit stressed and distracted .

Rohan, you've been staring off into space for the past ten minutes," Eeshan said, nudging him playfully. "What's on your mind? Or should I say, who's on your mind?"

Rohan chuckled, shaking his head. "I guess I'm just thinking about Myra. I haven't seen her in days, and it's driving me crazy. I just want the wedding to be here already so I can finally see her again."

Eeshan laughed, clapping Rohan on the back. "I get it, man. But don't worry, the big day is almost here. And after that, you two will have plenty of time to catch up. Especially on your honeymoon."

Rohan rolled his eyes, though he couldn't suppress a smile. "Leave it to you to bring up the honeymoon."

Eeshan grinned, clearly enjoying himself. "Well, someone has to make sure you're thinking ahead. Have you decided where you're taking her yet? Somewhere romantic, I hope."

Rohan smirked, his eyes twinkling with mischief. "I've got a few ideas. But I'm keeping it a surprise. Myra doesn't know where we're going, and I plan to keep it that way until the last minute."

Eeshan raised an eyebrow, impressed. "Nice move. Keeping her on her toes, huh? I like it."

The stressed atmosphere was eased down and now filled with teasing and laughter .

As the wedding day was approaching Myra found herself feeling a mix of emotions. She was excited, of course, but also a little nervous. There were so many details to take care of, and she wanted everything to be perfect. But every time she felt overwhelmed, she remembered Rohan's words: *As long as we're together, I'm ready for anything.*

One evening, after a particularly busy day, Myra was relaxing in her room when there was a soft knock on the door. Aashi poked her head in, holding a small envelope. "This just came for you," she said, handing it to Myra with a smile.

Myra took the envelope It was plain and unmarked, except for her name written in Rohan's handwriting. She felt a thrill of anticipation as she opened the envelope and unfolded the letter inside. Myra's hands trembled a little as she held it. She took a deep breath and began to read.

My Dearest Myra,

I wanted to write you this letter before the big day because there are some things I want to say that are hard to express in person. We've been so busy with the wedding preparations, and I know we haven't seen each other much these past few days. But you've been on my mind constantly.

First, I want to tell you how much you mean to me. Since the day I met you, my life has changed in the best possible way. You've brought so much happiness into my world, and I can't imagine my life without you in it. Every moment we've spent

together has been filled with love, laughter, and the kind of joy that makes life truly worth living.

As we get ready to start this new chapter of our lives, I want you to know that I'm committed to you, to us, and to our future together. I promise to be there for you, to support you in everything you do, and to love you with all my heart.

I know there will be challenges ahead, as there are in every relationship, but I believe that we can face anything as long as we're together. You are my best friend, my partner, and the love of my life. And I can't wait to see what the future holds for us.

Thank you for choosing me to be your partner. I promise to do everything I can to make you happy, to make our life together one filled with love, respect, and understanding. I am so excited to spend the rest of my life with you.

With all my love,

Rohan

Myra's eyes filled with tears as she read Rohan's words. She could feel the sincerity and love in every line, and it touched her deeply. She wiped away a tear and hugged the letter to her chest, overwhelmed by the love she felt for Rohan.

Aashi, who had been watching from the doorway, came over and put an arm around Myra. "Are you okay?" she asked gently.

Myra nodded, smiling through her tears. "I'm more than okay. I'm just... so happy. Rohan's words are so beautiful. I can't wait to marry him."

Aashi smiled and squeezed Myra's hand. "You deserve all the

happiness in the world, Myra. And Rohan's a great guy. You two are going to have an amazing life together."

Myra held the letter close and closed her eyes, picturing Rohan's face. She could almost feel him there with her, his warmth, his love. It made the days of waiting seem both shorter and longer at the same time. The anticipation of seeing him again, of finally being together, was almost too much to bear.

The preparations were almost complete, and soon, the day they had both been waiting for would arrive. Myra knew that no matter what, as long as she and Rohan were together, everything would be perfect.

18

THE BIG DAY

The long-awaited day had finally arrived. Myra and Rohan's wedding day was here, and the excitement in both their homes was beyond anything they had experienced before. It was a day filled with joy, love, and a bit of nervous energy as everyone prepared for the big event.

At Myra's house, the preparations were in full swing. Her room was a whirlwind of activity—women rushing in and out with trays of jewelry, makeup artists applying the final touches, and the scent of jasmine and rose filling the air. Myra sat in front of her mirror, her heartbeat racing . Today, she would become Rohan's wife.

Myra's bridal outfit had been the talk of the family ever since she had chosen it. Now, as she finally wore it, she felt every bit the bride she had always dreamed of being. Her lehenga was a deep, rich red—the traditional color for Indian brides. The fabric shimmered with gold embroidery, intricate and detailed, showing off patterns of flowers and delicate designs that caught the light in the most magical way. The skirt was heavy, with layers of fabric that moved gracefully as she adjusted her position. The blouse was equally stunning, with intricate embroidery and small mirrors that sparkled with every movement. The dupatta, a matching red veil with golden borders, was draped gracefully over her head, adding to the bridal look.

Her jewellery was just as breathtaking. Around her neck, she wore a gold necklace with small, sparkling diamonds, matching earrings, bangles that jingled softly with every movement and most importantly her engagement ring-that solitaire wrapped around her finger . Her wrists were adorned with a traditional red chooda, the set of bangles that every Indian bride wears, symbolizing love and prosperity. The chooda was bright red, with gold details, and as Myra looked at it, she felt a surge of emotion. This was a symbol of her new life, of the love she would share with Rohan for the rest of her days.

Her makeup was simple yet elegant, with soft shades of gold and brown on her eyes, a hint of blush on her cheeks, and a deep red lipstick that completed the look. Her hair was done up in a neat bun, with strands of jasmine woven into it, the fragrance adding to the aura of her grace and beauty . As she looked at herself in the mirror, she felt a mixture of happiness, excitement, and a bit of nervousness. This was the moment she had dreamed of, and now it was real. But in the midst of all the emotions, one thought stood out clearly — today, she would finally marry the love of her life.

Meanwhile, at Rohan's house, the atmosphere was just as charged. His friends and family bustled around him, helping him with the final touches of his wedding outfit. His sherwani, a traditional Indian groom's outfit, was an elegant ivory color, made of rich silk with gold embroidery that matched Myra's lehenga. The design was sophisticated and understated. He wore a matching turban, also in ivory and gold, with a small jewel in the center. Around his neck, he wore a long necklace made of pearls and gold, a traditional accessory that completed his royal look.

Rohan adjusted his sherwani in front of the mirror, feeling a sense of pride and excitement. His mother stood beside him, adjusting the turban with tears of joy in her eyes. "You look just like a prince, Rohan," she said, her voice filled with emotion. Rohan smiled, his heart swelling with happiness. But as much as he appreciated the compliments, his mind was elsewhere. He couldn't stop thinking about Myra. He hadn't seen her in a few days, and the anticipation of finally seeing her as his bride was almost too much to bear.

"Today is the day, Ma," he said softly, his voice tinged with a mix of excitement and nervousness. "I'm marrying the love of my life."

His mother smiled, placing a gentle hand on his shoulder. "She's a lucky girl, and you're a lucky man. The two of you are going to have a beautiful life together."

Rohan nodded, feeling a lump form in his throat. The reality of the moment was sinking in, and he was overwhelmed with emotion. He had waited for this day for so long, and now that it was here, it felt almost surreal.

As the preparations continued, Rohan's best friend, Eeshan, walked in with a teasing grin. "Well, well, look at you," he said, clapping Rohan on the back. "Ready to meet your bride , i hope you won't cry after seeing her - will you ?"

Rohan chuckled, but he knew Eeshan was right. The thought of seeing Myra walking down the aisle, dressed as a bride, was enough to bring tears to his eyes. "I might just do that," he admitted with a smile. "I can't even imagine how beautiful she's going to look."

"Just make sure you don't mess up your makeup," Eeshan teased, earning a laugh from Rohan. But behind all this , Rohan knew that today was going to be one of the most emotional days of his life.

As the time for the wedding ceremony approached, guests started to arrive at the venue. The decorators had transformed the space into something out of a fairy tale. The main area was filled with flowers—roses, marigolds, and jasmine—all arranged in beautiful patterns that filled the air with a sweet fragrance. The mandap, where the wedding ceremony would take place, was covered in red and gold drapes, with garlands of flowers hanging from the ceiling. Golden lanterns were placed all around, casting a warm, inviting glow over everything.

The atmosphere was lively, filled with the sound of laughter, music, and the clinking of bangles as everyone mingled and admired the beautiful decor.

As the ceremony drew closer, the excitement in the air grew. Myra, now fully ready, took a deep breath as Aashi, her best friend, came into the room. "It's time, Myra," Aashi said softly, her eyes shining with happiness.

Myra's heart skipped a beat. This was it. She was about to walk out and see Rohan, to finally marry him. Her emotions were a whirlwind—love, excitement, a little bit of nervousness—but above all, a deep sense of happiness. She looked at Aashi and smiled, her eyes brimming with tears. "I can't believe this is happening," she whispered.

Aashi took her hand and squeezed it gently. "You look beautiful, Myra. Rohan is going to lose his mind when he sees you."

Myra laughed softly, wiping away a tear. "I just want everything to be perfect."

"It already is," Aashi assured her. "Now, let's go make some memories."

The sound of the wedding song, "Din Shagna Da," began to play, signaling Myra's entrance. The soft, melodic tune filled the air, and the guests turned in anticipation. Myra, her heart pounding in her chest, began her walk down the aisle, each step bringing her closer to Rohan.

Rohan stood at the mandap, his eyes fixed on the entrance. As the first notes of "Din Shagna Da" filled the air, he felt his breath catch in his throat. And then, he saw her. Myra, his bride, dressed in a stunning red lehenga, her chooda adorning her wrists, her veil delicately framing her face. She looked like a vision, a dream come true.

Tears welled up in Rohan's eyes as he watched her walk towards him. He had always known Myra was beautiful, but today, she looked like an angel. His heart swelled with emotion, and for a moment, he felt like he might actually cry. But it wasn't just her beauty that moved him—it was the realization that this incredible woman was about to become his wife. The love he felt for her was overwhelming, and he knew in that moment that he would do anything to make her happy.

Myra, too, was overcome with emotion as she walked towards Rohan. She could see the tears in his eyes, and it made her heart ache with love. She had never seen him like this—so vulnerable, so full of love—and it made her love him even more. As she reached the mandap, Rohan extended his hand to her, and she took it, feeling a sense of peace wash over her. This was where she was meant to be, by his side, for the rest of her life.

The air was thick with emotion as Myra and Rohan exchanged garlands, a symbol of their acceptance of each other. As they placed the flowers around each other's necks, they couldn't help but smile, their eyes locked in a gaze .

As the ceremony continued, the time came for the pheras, the seven sacred rounds around the holy fire. Each round represented a vow, a promise they made to each other for their future life together. Myra and Rohan took the first step, their hands clasped together, their hearts full of love and commitment.

With each phera, they made a promise:

First Phera: As they circled the sacred fire, Myra's heart swelled with love, knowing that she would always have Rohan by her side, no matter what life threw at them. Rohan squeezed her hand gently, as if to say, "I will always take care of you."

Second Phera: They promised to grow together in strength and in wisdom. Myra could focus on was the warmth of Rohan's hand in hers, the steady presence that would guide her through life. She could see the determination in his eyes, a silent promise that he would always stand by her side, no matter what challenges they might face.

Third Phera: The third phera was a promise of faithfulness and respect. As they walked around the fire for the third time, Myra couldn't help but glance up at Rohan. His gaze met hers, filled with love and sincerity. In this moment, they both knew that their love would be unwavering, their respect for each other unshakable.

Fourth Phera : The fourth round represented their commitment to support each other in sickness and in health. Myra's thoughts drifted to the many years ahead, and she felt a deep sense of comfort knowing that Rohan would be there with her, through good times and bad.She knew, without a doubt, that they would face whatever challenges came their way, together.

Fifth Phera: In the fifth phera, they promised to care for and raise a family together. As they walked this round, Rohan's thoughts wandered to the future, imagining a home filled with laughter, and the joy of building a life together. He looked at Myra, envisioning her as the mother of their children, and he couldn't help but feel a rush of happiness. They were not just committing to each other, but also to the future they would create together — a family filled with love and happiness.

Sixth Phera: The sixth phera was a vow to always be each other's best friend. As they took this round, Myra smiled, thinking about all the times Rohan had been always her support system, and her closest companion. They had shared so much already, and this promise was a reminder that their friendship was the foundation of their love. They would always be there for each other, sharing secrets, dreams, and every small moment that life would bring.

Seventh Phera: The final round, the seventh phera, was a promise to always remain true to each other and to maintain the bond of love for eternity. As they walked this last circle around the fire, Rohan's eyes glistened with unshed tears. This was a vow to love each other endlessly, to be loyal and devoted for all time. When they completed the seventh round, they stood facing each other, their hands still clasped together and the room filled with the sounds of applause and cheers.

As the ceremony concluded, Myra and Rohan were surrounded by their loved ones, who showered them with blessings and well-wishes. The atmosphere was filled with joy, but for Myra and Rohan, the world seemed to narrow down to just the two of them. They were lost in each other's eyes, still holding hands, still wrapped up in the magic of the moment.

Aashi was the first to come up and embrace Myra, tears in her eyes. "You were beautiful, Myra. This was perfect."

Eeshan hugged Rohan tightly, slapping him on the back. "You did it, man. You married the love of your life. I'm so happy for you."

But despite the celebrations around them, Myra and Rohan could hardly tear their eyes away from each other. Rohan reached up, gently wiping away a tear that had escaped down Myra's cheek. "You were the most beautiful bride I've ever seen," he whispered, his voice thick with emotion.

"And you were the most handsome groom," Myra replied, her heart overflowing with love. "I still can't believe this is real."

Rohan smiled, his eyes shining with unshed tears. "It's real, Myra. We're married. You're mine, and I'm yours. Forever."

"Forever," Myra echoed, feeling the truth of the word settle deep in her heart.

The rituals continued with the Sindoor and Mangalsutra ceremony, where Rohan carefully applied a small amount of sindoor to Myra's forehead, right where her hair parted. The gesture was simple yet powerful, a mark of their marriage that Myra would carry with her always. Rohan then took the mangalsutra, a necklace made of black and gold beads with an infinity charm in between that explained their bond - *"to infinity and beyond "* , and placed it around Myra›s neck. This was another symbol of their union, one that would stay close to her heart for the rest of their lives.

As Rohan secured the mangalsutra, Myra looked up at him, her eyes full of love and gratitude. "Thank you, Rohan, for everything. For loving me, for choosing me."

Rohan smiled, his hand gently brushing against her cheek. "I didn't choose you, Myra. My heart did. And it was the best decision I ever made."

Throughout the night, Rohan couldn't take his eyes off Myra. Every time he looked at her, his heart swelled with love and pride. She was his wife now, and he was hers. The thought filled him with a deep sense of contentment and joy.

Rohan turned to Myra, his eyes soft with emotion. "I almost cried when I saw you walk down that aisle," he confessed, his voice barely above a whisper. "You took my breath away, Myra. I've never seen anything so beautiful."

Myra's heart melted at his words. "I felt the same when I saw you," she replied, her voice equally soft. "I couldn't believe that I was about to marry the man of my dreams."

Rohan smiled, his hand reaching up to caress her cheek. "This is just the beginning, Myra. We have a lifetime ahead of us, filled with love, laughter, and so many memories."

Myra nodded, leaning into his touch. "I can't wait to start this journey with you." - " *hand in hand you and me till the end* , « she added

As they stood there, wrapped in each other's arms, Rohan whispered the words that would forever stay in Myra's heart. "You are my everything, Myra. My love, my life, my forever."

And in that moment, Myra knew that she had found the greatest love of all — the love that would last a lifetime.

The night ended with a feeling of completeness, of two souls who had found their perfect match. Their journey had just begun, but they knew that no matter what the future held, they would face it together, hand in hand, heart to heart.

True love stories never have endings, but they do have beautiful beginnings. And this, Myra and Rohan knew, was the most beautiful beginning of all.

EPILOGUE

Months had passed since Myra and Rohan's wedding, and life had settled into a beautiful rhythm. Their days were filled with laughter, shared dreams, and the comfort of knowing they had each other to lean on, no matter what.

Their home, now filled with the warmth of love and the scent of fresh flowers, had become their little haven. Each room echoed with memories of their wedding day, a constant reminder of the vows they had made to each other. Myra often found herself smiling as she walked through the house, recalling the moments that had brought them to this point—their first meeting, the laughter they shared, the misunderstandings they overcame, and the love that only grew stronger with each passing day.

Rohan, too, couldn't believe how lucky he was. Every morning, he woke up beside the woman of his dreams, and every night, he fell asleep knowing that his heart had found its home. They were partners in every sense of the word—supporting each other, dreaming together, and building a life filled with love and happiness.

Their love story was not about grand gestures or dramatic moments; it was about the quiet, everyday moments that made their love special. It was in the way Rohan would make Myra a cup of tea without her asking, or the way Myra would rest her head on Rohan's shoulder when they watched a movie together. It was in the way they could spend hours talking about nothing and everything, or in the comfortable silence they shared when words weren't necessary.

As they looked forward to the future, Myra and Rohan knew that life would bring its share of challenges. But they also knew that they would face them together, hand in hand, just as they had promised on their wedding day. Their love was their strength, their guiding light, and they knew that as long as they had each other, they could overcome anything.

In the end, it wasn't the grand milestones that defined their love story, but the small, everyday moments that made their love grow stronger. They had found something truly special — a love that would last a lifetime.

And so, as the sun set on another day, Myra and Rohan sat together on their porch, watching the sky turn shades of pink and orange. Rohan gently took Myra's hand in his, their fingers intertwining, a silent promise that they would always be there for each other.

As they looked out at the horizon, Myra leaned her head on Rohan's shoulder, a content smile on her face. "I'm so happy, Rohan," she whispered, her voice filled with emotion.

Rohan kissed the top of her head, his heart full. "Me too, Myra. Me too."

And with that, they sat in peaceful silence, knowing that their love story, had become something beautiful, something lasting, something true.

"True love is not about the grand gestures or the dramatic moments; it's found in the quiet, everyday acts of love and understanding. In the end, it's the little things that make a love story timeless."

9 789395 034968